ETIQUETTE FOR LADIES:

A COMPLETE GUIDE TO

VISITING, ENTERTAINING, AND TRAVELLING,

WITH HINTS ON

COURTSHIP, MARRIAGE, AND DRESS.

LONDON:
WARD, LOCK, AND TYLER, WARWICK HOUSE,
PATERNOSTER ROW, E.C.

Published in Great Britain in 2011 by Old House books & maps,
Midland House, West Way, Botley, Oxford OX2 0PH, United Kingdom.
44-02 23rd Street, Suite 219, Long Island City, NY 11101, USA.
Website: www.oldhousebooks.co.uk

A CIP catalogue record for this book is available from the British Library.

ISBN-13: 978 1 90840 209 7

Originally published in 1876 by Ward, Lock & Tyler, Warwick House,
Paternoster Row, E.C.

Printed in China through Worldprint Ltd.

11 12 13 14 15 10 9 8 7 6 5 4 3 2 1

CONTENTS.

———

CONTENTS.

ETIQUETTE FOR LADIES.

MANNER IN THE STREET.

WHEN three ladies are walking together, it is better for one to keep a little in advance of the other two, than for all three to persist in maintaining one unbroken line. They cannot all join in conversation without talking across each other—a thing that, in-doors or out-of-doors, is awkward, inconvenient, ungenteel, and should always be avoided. Also, three ladies walking abreast occupy too much of the pavement, and, therefore, incommode the other passengers. If you meet a lady with whom you have become but slightly acquainted, and had merely a little conversation (for instance, at a party or a morning visit), and who moves in a circle somewhat higher or more fashionable than your own, it is proper to wait till she recognizes you. Let her not see in you a disposition to obtrude yourself on her notice.

It is not expected that all intimacies formed at watering-places should continue after the parties have returned to their homes. A mutual bow when meeting in the street is sufficient; but there is no interchanging of visits unless ladies have, before parting, testified a desire to continue the acquaintance. In this case the lady who is the senior, or palpably highest in station, makes the first call. It is not customary for a young lady to make the first visit to a married lady.

When meeting them in the street, always speak first to your milliner, mantua-maker, seamstress, or to any one you have been in the habit of employing. To pass without notice servants whom you know is rude and unfeeling, and they will attribute it to pride, not presuming to speak to you themselves unless in reply. There are persons who, having accepted, when in the country, much kindness from the country people, are ashamed to recognize them when they come to town on account of their rustic or unfashionable attire. This is vulgar and contemptible, and is always seen through and despised. Those to be avoided are such as wear tawdry finery, paint their faces and leer, looking graceless, even if they are not disreputable in reality. When meeting a gentleman whom a lady has no objection to numbering among her acquaintances, she denotes it by bowing first. If she has any reason to disapprove of his character or habits, she is perfectly justified in " cutting" him, as it is termed. Let her bow very coldly the first time, and after that not at all. When a lady is walking between two gentlemen she should divide her conversation as equally as practicable, or address most of it to the greater stranger to her. He to whom she is least on ceremony will excuse her. If you stop a few minutes in the street to talk to an acquaintance, draw to one side of the pavement, near the wall, so as not to impede the passengers, or you may turn and walk with her as far as the next corner. And never stop to talk in the middle of a crossing. To speak loudly in the street is unladylike, and to call across the way to an acquaintance is in execrable taste. It is best to hasten over and speak to her if you have anything of importance to say.

When a stranger offers to assist you over a puddle, or something of the kind, do not hesitate or decline as if you thought he was taking an unwarrantable liberty. He means nothing but civility ; so accept it frankly, and thank him for it.

On being escorted home by a gentleman a lady expects he will not leave her till he has rung the bell, and waited until she is actually in the house, although it has been thought sufficient, by men who know no better, to walk with her to the foot of the steps, and then take their departure, leaving her to get in as she can.

SHOPPING.

HEN visiting the shops, if you do not intend to buy at that time, but are merely looking round to see varieties of articles before you determine on what to purchase, candidly say so to the shopmen ; they will (particularly if they know you) be perfectly willing to show you such things as you desire to see, in the hope that you may return and buy of them afterwards.

At the same time avoid giving unnecessary trouble, and do not, from mere curiosity, desire such things to be brought as you have no intention of buying at all. If, however, you have given the salesman or saleswoman unusual trouble in showing you articles which will not suit your purpose, it is only right that you should make some compensation by, at least, one or two small purchases before leaving—a few articles that will always come into use.

The practice that is called cheapening, or beating down the price, is now nearly obsolete. Most tradesmen have a fixed price for everything, and will not abate. Yet there are still some ladies who think that one of the great arts of shopping is to disparage the articles shown to them, to exclaim at the price, and to assert that at other places they can get exactly such things infinitely lower. When shopping (as well as under all other circumstances) it is best to adhere to the truth. If you really like the article, why not gratify the salesman by saying so. If you know that the price is a fair one, you need not attempt to get it lower, for you will seldom succeed.

Shopping with a very close economist, particularly if you know that she can well afford a sufficiently liberal expenditure, is very trying. The length of time she will ponder over everything before she can "make up her mind," the ever-besetting fear that she may possibly have to give a few pence more in one shop than in another, her long deliberation as to whether a smaller than the usual quantity may not be "made to do," her predilection for bargain-seeking in streets far off, and the immense trouble she gives to the persons behind the counter, all will induce you to avoid a shopper who sets out with the vain expectation of obtaining good articles at paltry prices.

In what are called "cheap shops" you will rarely find more than two or three things that are really cheap. If of bad quality, they are not cheap, but dear. Low-priced ribbons. for instance, are generally flimsy, tawdry, of ugly figures, and vulgar colours—soon fading, and soon " getting into a string." Yet there are ladies who will walk two miles to hustle in the crowd they find squeezing toward the counter of the last new emporium of new ribbons ; and, while waiting their turn, have nothing to look at around them but lots of trash, which, if they bought, they would be ashamed to wear.

When on a visit to a city with which you are not familiar, inquire where the best shops are to be found, and take a note of them in your tablets. This will spare your friends the trouble of accompanying you on your shopping expeditions. Except to ladies whose chief delight is in seeing things connected with dress, to go shopping with a stranger is very tiresome. Also, the stranger will feel less constraint by going alone, and more at liberty to be guided by her own taste in selecting, and to consult her pecuniary convenience in regard to the price. It is only when you feel that you have reason for distrusting your own judgment as to the quality and style of the article that it is well to be accompanied by a person of more experience ; and then you will most probably be unwilling to fatigue her by going to as many shops as you would like to visit. In most cases it is best to go shopping without any companion, except, perhaps, a member of your immediate family. Gentlemen consider it a very irksome task to go on shopping expeditions, and their ill-concealed impatience becomes equally irksome to you.

When you see on another lady a new article of dress that you admire, it is not considered rude to tell her so. But, unless you really desire to get one exactly like it for yourself, and are sincerely asking for information, it is rude to inquire where she bought it and what she paid for it. And it is particularly vulgar to preface the inquiry by the foolish words,

5

"If it is a fair question." The very doubt proves that you know the question to be an unfair one; and so it is. The expression is seldom used except to introduce something rude and improper. Any lady who is asked an impertinent question would be perfectly justified in saying, "Excuse me from answering," and then immediately changing the conversation. Yet there are ladies who are always catechising others about their dress. You are not bound to give explicit answers to these or any other question concerning your personal affairs. Much mischief accrues in society by some ladies being too inquisitive and others too communicative.

If you meet an acquaintance unexpectedly in a shop, it is selfish to engage in a long conversation with her, and thus detain persons behind the counter from waiting on other customers. Finish your purchase-making first, and then you will have leisure to step aside and converse. A shop is hardly a suitable place for social intercourse, and you may say something there that bystanders should not hear. Interfering with the shopping of other customers, who may be standing near you at the counter, by either praising or deprecating any of the articles they are looking at, is a piece of gratuitous impertinence. Leave them to the exercise of their own judgment, however faulty it may be, unless they ask your opinion; and then give it in a low voice and sincerely. It is not admissible to try on kid gloves in a shop. After buying a pair ask for the glove-stretcher (which is kept in all good shops for the convenience of customers), and then stretch the gloves upon it, unless you have a glove-stretcher at home.

If a lady is expected to display good taste and good sense in shopping, the saleswomen who attend upon her should, when commencing their vocation, have cultivated two important qualities—civility and patience. Moreover, activity in moving and quickness in recollecting where all the articles called for are to be found, so as not to keep the customers waiting too long while they, the sellers, are searching the shelves and boxes. Also, if a lady wishes to match something it is foolish and useless to bring her a piece that is not exactly like, trying to persuade her to take it, and calling it " as good a match as she is likely to get." Of course she will not take a piece that is only tolerably like, but not quite the same ; for, unless it matches exactly, it is no match at all.

As much civility and attention should be shown to a customer plainly dressed and walking on foot as to a lady elegantly attired and coming in her own carriage. The former may prove the most profitable customer. Be careful to exhibit no signs of irritation, even if you have had the trouble of showing a variety of goods to one who goes away without buying anything ; another time, perhaps, she may come and make large purchases, but if you offend her she will assuredly never enter the shop again. Recollect that no one feels under the least compulsion to buy what does not suit them. You would not yourself. Habitual courtesy is a valuable qualification, and always turns to good account.

LADIES AT PLACES OF AMUSEMENT.

O secure a good seat at any place of amusement go early. It is better to sit an hour before the performance begins than to arrive after it has commenced. The time of waiting will soon pass away in conversation with the friends whom you have accompanied. When practicable, leave bonnets, hats, cloaks, and hoods in the apartment set apart for ladies, as it is very painful and fatiguing for those behind moving the head from side to side, and stretching the neck this way and that, and peeping wherever a tantalizing glimpse can be obtained between the hats or bonnets of ladies seated immediately in front. This, in addition to the annoyance of being squeezed on a bench that is over full, is enough to destroy nearly all the pleasure of the evening.

When invited to join a party begin to prepare in ample time, so as not to keep them waiting for you. When a *large* party is going to a place of amusement (for instance, the theatre or opera) it is better that each family should go thither from their own home (being provided with their own tickets),

8

than that they should all rendezvous at the house of one of the company, at the risk of keeping the whole party waiting perhaps for the very youngest members of it. When a box has been taken, let.the tickets be sent to all the persons who are to have seats in it, and not retained by the taker of the box till the whole party have assembled at the door of the theatre. If the tickets are thus distributed, the persons from each house can go when they please without compelling any of the party to wait for them.

To make an entrance after the performance has begun is (or ought to be) very embarrassing to ladies. It excites the attention of all around, diverting attention from the performance ; and there is always, when the house is full and the hour late, some delay and difficulty in reaching the seats even when they have been engaged.

If it is a concert, where places cannot be previously secured, there are of course additional reasons for going in due time, and the most sensible and best-behaved part of the audience always endeavour to do so. But if you are unavoidably late be satisfied to pay the penalty by quietly taking back seats, if no others are vacant. Young ladies arriving after the performance had commenced, have been seen walking boldly up to the front benches and standing there looking steadfastly in the faces of gentlemen who, with their parties, had earned good seats by coming soon after the doors were opened. The ladies persevered in this determined stare till they succeeded in dislodging these unfortunate gentlemen, and compelling them to quit their seats, to leave the ladies of their party, and stand for the remainder of the evening in a distant part of the room.

To laugh deridingly or to whisper unfavourable remarks during the performance of a concert or a play is a rudeness of which no English lady is guilty. Occasionally are seen

9

some of that few who, much to the annoyance of those persons near them who really wish to enjoy what they came for, talk audibly in ridicule of the performers, the performers being, in all probability, near enough to hear these vexatious remarks, and to be disconcerted by them. It is also a gross breach of good breeding to anticipate the "good things," or destroy the interest of others in the plot of the piece by stating what you may know of either, to those near you.

AT CHURCH.

Ladies should endeavour always to be in their pews before the service begins, and when the Benediction is finished take their departure quietly, without any hurry or bustle. If you go into a church where you are a stranger, wait in the vestibule until you see the sexton, and then request him to show you a vacant seat. This is better than to wander about the aisles alone, or to intrude yourself into a pew where you may cause inconvenience to its owners. If you see that a pew is full you know of course that you cannot obtain a seat in it without dislodging somebody. If a family invites you to go to church with them or to come thither, and to have a seat in their pew, do not take the liberty of asking a friend of your own to accompany you; and, above all, do not bring a child with you. Should you (having a pew of your own) ask another lady to go with you, call for her in due time, and she ought to be quite ready. Place her in a corner seat (it being the most comfortable), and see that she is accommodated with a footstool; and be assiduous in finding the places for her in the prayer book or hymn book.

In visiting a church of a different denomination from your own, comply as far as you can with all the ceremonies observed by the congregation, particularly if you are in a foreign country. Even if some of these observances are not the least in conformity with your own opinions and feelings, remember that you are there as a guest and have no right to offend or displease your hosts by evincing a marked disapprobation of their mode of worship. If you find it very irksome to refrain (which it should not be) you need not go a second time.

Young ladies who, on their way to church, laugh and talk loudly with their escort are, to say the least, guilty of a serious indiscretion. It is too probable that their escort will occupy a large share of their thoughts during the hours of worship. Nay, there are some so irreverent and so regardless of the sanctity of the place as to indulge in frequent whispers to those near them, or to their friends in adjoining pews.

SUGGESTIONS TO VISITORS.

THE ENTRÉE.

A LADY is said to have the *entrée* of her friend's room when she is allowed or assumes the privilege of entering it familiarly at all times, and without any previous intimation—a privilege too often abused. In many cases the visited person has never really granted this privilege (and after growing wise by experience she rarely will), but the visitor, assuming that she herself must under all circumstances be welcome, carries her sociability so far as to become troublesome and inconvenient.

There are few occasions on which it is proper, on entering a house, to run directly to the chamber of your friend, and to enter her room without knocking, or the very instant after knocking, before she has time to desire you to enter or to make the slightest arrangement for your reception. You may find her washing or dressing, or even engaged in repairing clothes—or the room may be in great disorder, or the chambermaid in the act of cleaning it. No one likes unseasonable interruptions, even from a very dear friend.

A familiar visit will always begin more pleasantly if the visitor inquires of the servant at the door if the lady she wishes to see is at home, and then goes into the parlour and stays there until she has sent her name, and ascertained that she can be received upstairs. Then, and not till then, let her go to her friend's room, taking care to knock before entering.

It is extremely rude, on being admitted to a private apartment, to look curiously about as if taking an inventory of all that is to be seen. We have known ladies whose eyes were all the time gazing round, and even slily peering under tables, sofas, &c., turning their heads to look after every person who chanced to move about the room, and giving particular attention to whatever seemed to be in disorder or out of place.

Make no remark upon the work in which you find your friend engaged. If she lays it aside, desire her not to leave it because of your presence, but propound no questions concerning it. Do not look over her books, and ask to borrow them. In short, meddle with nothing.

If you are perfectly certain that you have really the *entrée* of your friend's room, you have no right ever to extend that privilege to any other person who may chance to be with you when you go to see her. It is taking an unjustifiable liberty to intrude a stranger upon the privacy of her chamber. If another lady is with you waive the privilege of *entrée* for that time, take your companion into the parlour, and send up the names of both.

There are certain unoccupied ladies so over-friendly as to take the *entrée* of the whole house. These are generally ultra-neighbourly neighbours, who run in at all hours of the day and evening ; ferret out the ladies of the family wherever they may be ; watch their proceedings when engaged like good housewives in inspecting the attics, the store rooms, the cellars, or the kitchen. Never for a moment do they seem to suppose that their hourly visits may perhaps be inconvenient or unseasonable ; or too selfish to abate their frequency even when they suspect them to be so these inveterate sociablists make their incursions at all avenues. They are quite domesticated in your house. They see all, hear all, know all your concerns. Their talk *to* you is chiefly gossip, and therefore their talk *about* you is chiefly the same. They are *au fait* of everything concerning your table. They find out everybody that comes to your house ; know all your plans for going to this place or that ; are well acquainted with every article you wear ; are present at the visits of all your friends, and hear all their conversation. Their own is usually " an infinite deal of nothing."

To avoid the danger of being overwhelmed by the sociability of an idle neighbour, discourage the first indications of undue intimacy by making your own visits rather few and far between. A young lady of good sense and of proper self-respect will never be too lavish of her society ; and if she has pleasant neighbours will visit them always in moderation.

VISITING FRIENDS IN TOWN OR COUNTRY.

VISITING FRIENDS IN THE TOWN OR COUNTRY.

I T is hardly wise to volunteer a visit to a friend in the country or in another town, unless you have had what is called "a standing invitation," with every reason to believe that it was sincerely and cordially given. Many invitations are mere "words of course," without meaning or motive, designed only to make a show of politeness, and not intended to be taken literally, or ever acted upon. Even when convinced that your friend is really your friend, and will be happy in your society, it is best to apprize her duly of the exact day and hour when she may expect you; always with the proviso if it be convenient to herself to receive you at that time, and desiring her to let you know candidly if it is not. However close your intimacy, an unexpected arrival may possibly produce inconvenience to your hostess; particularly if her family is numerous, and her bed-rooms are few. The case is somewhat different where

15

the house is large, and where there is no scarcity of apartments for guests, of servants to wait upon them, or of money
to furnish the means of entertaining them liberally. But even
then, the time of arrival should be previously intimated and
observed as punctually as possible. When visits are attempted
as "agreeable surprises," they are seldom very agreeable to
the surprised.

Having received an invitation, reply to it immediately ; and
do not keep your friends waiting, day after day, in uncertainty
whether you mean to accept or decline it.

Excuse yourself from accepting invitations from persons
whom you do not like, and whose disposition, habits, feelings,
and opinions, are in most things the reverse of your own.
There can be no pleasure in daily and familiar intercourse
where there is no geniality. Such visits never end well ; and
they sometimes produce irreconcilable quarrels, or at least a
lasting and ill-concealed coolness. Though for years you may
have always met on decent terms, you may become positive
enemies, from living a short time under the same roof ; and
there is something dishonourable in laying yourself under
obligations, and receiving civilities from persons whom you
secretly dislike, and in whose society you can have little or no
enjoyment.

When you arrive, take occasion to mention how long you
intend to stay, that your hostess may plan her arrangements
accordingly. It is rude and inconsiderate to keep her in
ignorance of the probable duration of your visit. And when
the allotted time has expired, do not be persuaded to extend
it further unless you are earnestly and with undoubted sincerity
invited to do so. It is much better that your friends should
part with you reluctantly than you should give them reason to
wish your visit shorter. Even if it has been very pleasant on
both sides it may not continue so if prolonged too far.

On your first evening inquire the hours of the house that you may always be ready to comply with them. Rise early enough to be washed and dressed in time for breakfast; but if you are ready too early remain in your own apartment, or walk about the garden, or go to the library, till the cleaning or arranging of the sitting-room has been completed. Notwithstanding all that may be said to you about " feeling yourself

perfectly at home," and considering your friend's house as your own, be very careful not to do so literally. In fact, it is impossible you should with any propriety—particularly if it is your first visit. You cannot know the real character and disposition of any acquaintance till after you have had some experience in living under the same roof. If you find your hostess all that you can desire, and that she is making your

visit every way agreeable, be very grateful to her, and let he
understand that you are exceedingly happy at her house ; but
avoid staying too long or taxing her kindness too highly.

Avoid encroaching unreasonably upon your friend's time.
Expect her not to devote an undue portion of it to you. She
will probably be engaged in the superintendence of household
affairs, or in the care of her young children, for two or three
hours after breakfast. So at these hours do not intrude upon
her, but amuse yourself with some occupation of your own till
you see that it is convenient to the family for you to join them
in the sitting-room. In summer afternoons retire for an hour,
or more, soon after dinner, to your own apartment, that you
may give your friends an opportunity of taking a nap or resting
alone.

It is an advantage to be able to assist in entertaining your
entertainers. A silent visitor, whether silent from dullness or
indolence, or a habit of taciturnity, is never an agreeable one.
Yet, however pleasant the conversation, have sufficient self-
lenial to break off in reasonable time, so as not to keep the
family up by continuing in the parlour till a late hour.

While you are a guest at the house of a friend, do not pass
too much of your time in visiting at other houses unless she is
with you. You have no right to avail yourself of the con-
veniences of eating and sleeping at her house without giving
her and her family the largest portion of your company.

While a guest yourself, it is taking an unwarrantable liberty
to invite any of your friends or relatives to come there and
spend a day or days.

Refrain from visiting any person with whom your hostess is
not upon good terms, even if that person has been one of your
intimate friends. You will in all probability be regarded as
"a spy in the camp." There is nothing so difficult as to
observe a strict neutrality. The friend whose hospitality you

are enjoying will soon begin to look coldly upon you if she finds you seeking the society of her enemy; and she may evince that coldness whenever you come home from these visits. If you understand soon after your arrival that there is no probability of a reconciliation, send at once a concise note to the lady with whom your hostess is at variance; express your regret at the circumstance, and excuse yourself from visiting her while you remain in your present residence. This note should be polite, short, and decisive, and so worded as to give no offence to either side; for, before sending, it is proper for you to shew it, while yet unsealed, to the friend with whom you are staying. And then let the correspondence be carried no further. The lady to whom it is addressed will, of course, return a polite answer such as you may show to your hostess.

It is to be presumed that she will not be so lost to all delicacy and propriety as to intrude herself into the house of her enemy for the purpose of visiting you. But if she does, it is your place civilly to decline seeing her. A slight-coolness, a mere offence on a point of etiquette, which, if let alone, would die out like a tender spark, has been fanned and blown into a flame by the what may be called go-betweening of a mutual friend. It is unkind and disrespectful to the family with whom you are staying to hold intercourse with any enemy of the house, and perhaps unsafe for yourself.

If you know that your friends are hurried with their sewing, &c., or with preparations for company, offer to assist them as far as you can. But if you are conscious of an incapacity to do such things well, it is better to excuse yourself by candidly saying so than to attempt them and spoil them.

When called on by any of your own acquaintance, they will not expect you to ask them to stay tea or to dinner. That is the business of your hostess, not yours.

It is proper for visitors to put out and pay for their own washing, ironing, &c. Therefore, carry among your baggage two clothes-bags, one to be taken away by the laundress, the other to receive your clothes in the interval.

Take with you a small writing-case, containing whatever stationery you may be likely to want during your visit, including postage stamps. Thus you will spare yourself and spare the family the inconvenience of applying to them whenever you have occasion for pen, ink, paper, &c. Also take care to be well supplied with all sorts of sewing articles. There are young ladies who go from home on long visits quite unprovided with even thimbles and scissors, depending all the time on borrowing. Many visitors, though very agreeable in great things, are exceedingly troublesome in little ones.

On concluding your visit, tell your entertainers that it has been pleasant, and express your gratitude for the kindness you have received from them, and the hope that they will give you an opportunity of returning their civilities. Give a parting gratuity to each of the servants—the sum being according to your means and to the length of your visit.

After reaching home, write very soon (within two or three days) to the friend at whose house you have been staying, telling her of your journey, &c., and allude to your visit as having been very agreeable. The visit over, be of all things careful not to repeat anything that has come to your knowledge which your late entertainers would wish to remain unknown. While an inmate of their house you must have unavoidably become acquainted with some particulars of their way of living not generally known, and which, perhaps, would not raise them in public estimation if disclosed. Having been their guest and partaken of their hospitality, you are bound, in honour, to keep silent on every topic that would injure them in the smallest degree, if repeated. Whatever painful discoveries are made during a visit should be kept as closely secret as if secrecy was enjoined by oath. It is not sufficient to refrain from "mentioning names." No clue should be given that could possibly enable the hearers even to hazard a guess.

VISITS OF CEREMONY, FRIENDSHIP, AND CONDOLENCE.

O friends or very intimate acquaintance visits may be left to create their own etiquette, as, in fact, they *are* left, whatever rules may be laid down. Not to go too frequently to the same house; not to stay too long when you do go; to let no intimacy overstep the bounds of courtesy, are obvious hints. Half-an-hour amply suffices for a visit of ceremony. The lady may not remove any article of her attire, even if politely requested to do so by the mistress of the house. If, however, your visit is to a particular friend, the case is different; even then, it is best to wait till you are invited to do so.

21

Favourite dogs are never welcome visitors in a drawing room. Many people have even a dislike to such animals; they require watching lest they should leap upon a chair or sofa, or place themselves on a lady's dress, and attentions of the kind are much out of place. Neither ought a mother, when paying a ceremonial visit, to be accompanied by young children. It is frequently difficult to amuse them, and if not particularly well-trained at home, they naturally seize hold of books or those elegant ornaments with which it is fashionable to decorate the drawing-room. In some families evening calls are allowed. Should you chance to visit such a family, and find that they have a party, present yourself and converse for a few minutes with an unembarrassed air, after which you may retire, unless urged to remain. A slight invitation given for the sake of courtesy ought not to be accepted. Make no apology for your unintentional intrusion; but let it be known in the course of a few days that you were not aware that your friends had company.

Morning visits are usually paid between the hours of two and four p.m. in winter, and two and five in summer. The object in view in observing this rule is to avoid intruding before the luncheon is removed, and leave in sufficient time to allow the lady of the house leisure for her dinner toilette.

Should the lady you desire to call upon be from home, leave your card; no message is requisite. If your visit is intended for two persons, leave two cards. Do not turn down the corner of your card; that fashion has now exploded.

When introduced to strangers, bow slightly and enter at once into conversation with them; to bow and take no further notice of them, but to continue your conversation with the lady on whom you are calling, is a great want of good breeding. Visits of congratulation should be short, and must always be made before dinner.

Visits of condolence are to be paid with as little delay as possible after the occurrence which calls them forth. Unless you are very intimate, it is an evidence of better taste to leave a card than to intrude upon private sorrow. Should you be so nearly related as to render a personal visit necessary, take care to appear in a *quiet* dress, and if the occasion be the death of a person even slightly related to you, go in mourning—deep or otherwise, according to the degree of relationship. It is considered in good taste for ladies to make their calls in black silk or plain coloured apparel. It denotes that they sympathize with the afflictions of the family, and such attentions are always pleasing.

Cards must be left on all occasions of a formal character. A lady leaves her own, and two of her husband's—one is intended for the gentleman of the house and one for the lady. The names of a lady's daughters are often printed on the same card with the name of their mother, and when such a card is left, it implies that mother and daughters have called.

When you arrive in town it is proper to call and leave your card, as an intimation that you are in the neighbourhood, thus acting the reverse of what is considered polite when in the country, where the rule is that the stranger waits until called upon.

If the cards are left preparatory to leaving town the initials, P. P. C. (*pour prendre congé*) should be written in pencil on the corner of them. Sometimes when the departure is a hurried one, the cards may be sent by a servant; but it is better to call in person.

Cards sent during the illness of a member of a family should be accompanied by verbal inquiries as to the patient's state.

It is usual to send them twice or thrice a week for two weeks to the house of a lady the birth of whose child has been publicly announced.

Cards may be left or sent the day after a ball. If the house is in the country at which the ball was, the cards may be sent by post, but recourse should not be had to this medium where it can be avoided. After a dinner party, or a small party, cards should be left within a week.

A lady's card may be either glazed or plain. Some people omit the prefix " Miss " to their names on the card. This is an affectation of simplicity which takes away all appearance of that quality. It is a thing unknown in English society, though the fashion on the Continent, for a lady to have only her Christian name and her surname on the card.

The Visited.—Having invited a friend to pass a few days or weeks at your house, and expecting her at a certain time, meet her on arrival, or, if that be impracticable, send a servant to secure a conveyance and attend to her luggage. It is to be supposed that before her arrival you have inspected the chamber of your guest, to see that none of the articles that are in all genteel and well-furnished houses are wanting—that there are two pitchers of fresh water on the stand, and three towels on the rail (two fine and one coarse), a foot-bath, and other requisites. On the mantel-piece a candle or lamp, with a box of lucifer matches beside it—the candle to be replaced by a new one every morning when the chamber-maid arranges the room, or the lamp to be trimmed daily ; so that the visitor may have a light at hand whenever she pleases, without ringing the bell and waiting till a servant brings one up.

The room should have an easy chair with a foot cushion before it ; a low chair also, to sit on when shoes and stockings are to be changed, &c.

Let the centre table be furnished with a writing-desk, well supplied with all that is necessary ; also some books, such as you think your friend would like. Let her find, at least, one bureau vacant, all the drawers empty, so that she may be able to unpack her muslins, &c., and arrange them at once.

Arriving at your house, have your guest's baggage taken at once to the apartment prepared for her, and, when she goes upstairs, send a servant with her to unstrap her trunks. Then let her be left alone to arrange her dress.

Every morning after the chamber-maid has done her duty (the room of the visitor is the first to be put in order), the hostess should go in to see that all is right. This done, no further inspection is necessary. It is very kind and considerate to inquire of your guest if there is any dish or article of food that she particularly likes, so that you may have it on the table while she stays, and also if there is anything peculiarly disagreeable to her, so that you may refrain from having it during her visit.

For such deficiencies as may be avoided or remedied, refrain from making the absurd apology that you consider her "no stranger," and that you regard her "just as one of the family." If you invite her at all, it is your duty for your own sake as well as hers to treat her well in everything.

If she desires to assist you in sewing, and has brought no work of her own, you may avail yourself of the offer, and employ her in moderation—but let it be in moderation only, and when sitting in the family circle. When alone in her own room she, of course, would much rather read, write, or occupy herself in some way for her own benefit or amusement.

Let the children be strictly forbidden to run into the apartments of visitors; interdict them from going thither unless sent with a message, and then let them be made to understand that they are always to knock at the door, and not go in till desired to do so. Also that they are not to play and make a noise in the neighbourhood of her room. And when she comes into the parlour, that they are not to jump on her lap, put their hands into her pockets, or rummage her work-basket, or rumple and soil her dress by clinging to it with their hands. Neither should they be permitted to amuse themselves by rattling on the lower keys when she is playing on the piano, or interrupt her by teasing her all the time to play "for them to dance." To permit children to ask visitors for pennies or sixpences is mean and contemptible. And if money is given them by a guest, they should be made to return it immediately.

Inquire on the first evening if your visitor is accustomed to taking any refreshment before she retires for the night. If she is, have something sent up to her room every night, unless your own family are in the same habit. These little repasts are very pleasant, especially at the close of a long winter evening, and after coming home from a place of public amusement.

To "welcome the coming—speed the parting guest"—is a good maxim. So, when your visitor is about to leave you, make all smooth and ready for her departure. Let her be called up at an early hour if she is to set out in the morning. Send a servant up to strap and bring down her trunks, as soon as she has announced that they are ready; and see that an early breakfast is prepared for her, and some of the family up and dressed to share it with her. Have a cab or carriage at the door in due time, and let some male member of the family accompany her to the starting-place and see her off, attending to her baggage, and procuring tickets.

TEA VISITORS.

HEN you have invited a friend to take tea with you endeavour to render her visit as agreeable as you can ; and try by all means to make her comfortable.

The servant who attends the door should be instructed to show the guest upstairs as soon as she arrives, conducting her to an unoccupied apartment, where she may take off her bonnet and arrange her hair, or any part of her dress that may require change or improvement. The lady should then be left to herself. Nothing is polite that can possibly incommode or embarrass—therefore it is a mistaken civility for the hostess, or some female member of the family, to follow the visitors upstairs, and remain with her all the time she is preparing for her appearance in the parlour. Over-officiousness is not politeness, and nothing troublesome and inconvenient is ever agreeable.

The toilet-table should be always well furnished with a clean hair brush and a nice comb ; a hand-mirror of sufficient size to afford a glimpse of the back of the head anp neck. A small work-box, properly furnished with needles, scissors, thimble and thread, ought to find a place on the dressing-table, in case the visitor may have occasion to repair any accident that may have happened to her dress.

28

TEA VISITORS.

The hostess should be in the parlour prepared to receive her visitor, and to give her at once a seat in the corner of a sofa, or on a fauteuil, or large comfortable chair; if a rocking-chair, a footstool is an indispensable appendage. But rocking-chairs are now seldom seen in a parlour; handsome, stuffed easy chairs that are moved on castors are substituted.

If in consequence of dining very late you are in the habit of also taking tea at a late hour—or making but slight preparation for that repast—waive that custom when you expect a friend whom you know to be in the practice of dining early, and who, perhaps, has walked far enough to feel fatigued and to acquire an appetite. For her accommodation order the tea earlier than usual, and let it be what may be called a substantial tea. If there is ample room at table, do not have the tea carried round, particularly if you have but one servant to hand the whole. It is tedious, inconvenient, and unsatisfactory. The absurd practice of eating in gloves has been wisely abolished among genteel people.

Do not, in sitting down to table, inform your guest that "you make no stranger of her," or that you fear she will not be able to enjoy your "plain fare." These apologies are ungenteel and foolish. If your circumstances will not allow you on any consideration to make a little improvement in your usual family-fare, your friend is, in all probability, aware of the fact, and will not wish or expect you to incur any inconvenient expense on her account. But if you are known to possess the means of living well, you ought to do so; and to consider a good though not an extravagantly luxurious table as a necessary part of your expenditure. There is a vast difference between laudable economy and mean economy; the latter (whether it shows itself in bad food, bad fires, bad lights, bad servants) is never excused in persons who dress extravagantly and live surrounded by costly furniture, and who are known to be wealthy and able to afford comfort as well as show.

If you invite a friend to tea in whose own family there is no gentleman or no man-servant, it is your duty previously to ascertain that you can provide her on that evening with an escort home. If you keep a carriage, it will be most kind to send her home in it.

In inviting a few friends, which means a small, select company, endeavour to bring together people who have community of tastes, feelings and ideas. If you mix the dull and stupid with the bright and animated, the cold and formal with the frank and lively, the professedly serious with the gay and cheerful, the light with the heavy, and above all, those who pride themselves on their birth with those who boast of "belonging to the people;" none of these "few friends" will enjoy each other's society—the evening will not go off agreeably, and you and the other members of your family will have the worst of it. The pleasantest people in the room will naturally congregate together, and the task of entertaining the unentertainable will devolve on yourself and your own people.

If a friend makes an afternoon call, and you wish her to stay and take tea, invite her to do so at once, as soon as she has sat down, and do not wait until she has risen to depart. Should chance visitors come in before the family have gone to tea, let them at once be invited to partake of that repast, which they will, of course, decline, if they have had tea already. In a well-provided house there can be no difficulty in adding something to the family tea-table, which, in genteel life, should never be discreditably parsimonious. It is a very mean practice for the members of the family to slip out of the parlour one by one at a time and steal into an adjoining room to avoid inviting their visitor to accompany them. How much better to meet the inconvenience by conducting your accidental guest to the table, unless she says she has already taken tea, and will amuse herself with a book while the family are at theirs.

Casual evening visitors should avoid staying too late. Ten o'clock is the usual time to depart, or at least to prepare for doing so. If the visit is unduly prolonged, there may be evident signs of irrepressible drowsiness in the heads of the family, which, when perceived, will annoy the guest, who must then feel that she has stayed too long.

If you are engaged to take tea with an intimate friend, who assures you that you will see none but the family, and you afterwards receive an invitation to join a party to a place of amusement, which you have long been desirous of visiting, you may retract your first engagement, provided you send an apology in due time, telling the exact truth, and telling it in polite terms. Your intimate friend will then take no offence, considering it perfectly natural that you should prefer the concert, the play, or the exhibition, to a quiet evening passed at her house with no other guests. But take care to let her know as early as possible. And be careful not to disappoint her again in a similar manner.

CONVERSATION.

O form a perfect conversationist many qualifications are requisite. There must be knowledge of the world, knowledge of books, and a facility of imparting that knowledge; together with originality, memory, an intuitive perception of what is best to say, and best to omit, good taste, good temper, and good manners. An agreeable and instructive talker has the faculty of going "from grave to gay, from lively to severe," without any apparent effort, neither skimming so slightly over a variety of topics as to leave no impression of any, or dwelling so long upon one subject as to weary the attention of the hearers. Persons labouring under a monomania such as absorbs their whole mind into one prevailing idea, are never pleasant or impressive talkers. They defeat their own purpose by recurring to it perpetually, and rendering it a perpetual fatigue. A good talker should cultivate a temperance in talking, so as not to talk too much to the exclusion of other good talkers. Conversation is dialogue, not monologue.

To be a perfect conversationist, a good voice is indispensable —a voice that is clear, distinct, and silver-toned. If you find that you have a habit of speaking too low, "reform it altogether." It is a bad one, and will render your talk unintelligible.

Few things are more delightful than for one intelligent and well-stored mind to find itself in company with a kindred spirit—each understanding the other, catching every idea and comprehending every allusion. Such persons will become as intimate in half an hour as if they had been personally acquainted for years.

On the other hand, the pleasure of society is much lessened by the habit in which many persons indulge of placing themselves always in opposition, controverting every opinion, and doubting every fact. They talk to you as a lawyer examines a witness at the bar; trying to catch you in some discrepancy that will invalidate your testimony, fixing their scrutinizing eyes upon your face, and scarcely permitting you to say, ' It is a fine day," without making you prove your words. Such people are never popular. Nobody likes perpetual contradiction, especially when the subject of the argument is of little or no consequence. In young people this dogmatic practice is generally based upon vanity and impertinence. In the old it is prompted by pride and selfishness.

Unless he first refers to it himself, never talk to a gentleman concerning his profession ; at least do not question him about it. For instance, you must not expect a physician to tell you how his patients are affected or to confide to you any particulars of their maladies. These are subjects that he will discuss only with their relatives or their nurses. It is also very improper to ask a lawyer about his clients, or the cases in which he is employed. A clergyman does not like always to be talking about the church. A merchant, when away from his counting-house, has no wish to engage in business talk with ladies, and a mechanic is ever willing "to leave the shop behind him." Still, there are some few individuals who like to talk of their "bread-winner." If you perceive this disposition, indulge them and listen attentively. You will learn something useful and worth remembering.

Women who have begun the world in humble life, and have been necessitated to give most of their attention to household affairs, are generally very shy in talking of housewifery, after their husbands have become rich and are living in style, as it is called. Therefore do not annoy them by questions on domestic economy, but converse as if they had never known other circumstances.

Never remind any one of the time when their situation was less genteel or less affluent than at present, or tell them that you remember their living in a small house or in a remote street. If they have not moral courage to talk of such things themselves, it is rude in you to make any allusion to them.

On the other hand, if invited to a fashionable house and to meet fashionable company, it is not the time or place for you to set forth the comparative obscurity of your own origin by way of showing that you are not proud. If *you* are not proud, it is most unlikely that your entertainers will be pleased at your ultra-magnanimity in thus lowering yourself before their aristocratic guests. These communications should be reserved for *tête-à-têtes* with old and familiar friends who have no more pride than yourself.

When listening to a circumstance that is stated to have actually occurred to the relater, even if it strike you as being very extraordinary and not in conformity with your own

34

experience, it is rude to reply, "Such a thing never happened to me." It is rude, because it seems to imply a doubt of the narrator's veracity, and it is foolish because its not having happened to you is no proof that it could not have happened to anybody else. Slowness in belief is sometimes an evidence of ignorance rather than of knowledge. People who have read but little, travelled but little, and seen but little of the world out of their own immediate circle, and whose intellect is too obtuse to discern any new accession to their own small stock of ideas, are apt to think that nothing can be true unless it has fallen under their own limited experience.

When you hear a gentleman speak in praise of a lady whom you do not think deserving of his commendations, you will gain nothing by attempting to undeceive him, particularly if she is handsome. Your dissenting from his opinion he will in all probability impute to envy or ill-nature, and therefore the only impression you can make will be against yourself. Even if you have reason to dislike the lady, recollect that few are without some good points, both of person and character, and it will be much better for you to pass over her faults in silence, and agree with him in commending what is really commendable about her. What he would perhaps believe implicitly if told to him by a man he would attribute entirely to jealousy, or to a love of detraction, if related by a woman. Above all, if a gentleman descants on the beauty of a lady, and in your own mind you do not coincide with his opinion, refrain on your part from criticizing invidiously her face and figure, and do not say that "though her complexion may be fine, her features are not regular," that "her nose is too small," or "her eyes too large," or "her mouth too wide." Still less disclose to him the secret of her wearing false hair, artificial teeth, or tinging her cheeks with rouge.

If a foreigner chances in your presence to make an

unfavourable remark upon some custom or habit peculiar to your country, do not immediately take fire and resent it, for, perhaps, upon reflection you may find that he is right, or nearly so. All countries have their national character, and no character is perfect whether that of a nation or an individual. If you know that the stranger has imbibed an erroneous impression, you may calmly, and in a few words, endeavour to convince him of it. But if he shows an unwillingness to be convinced, and tells you that what he has said he heard from good authority, it will be worse than useless for you to continue the argument. Therefore change the subject, or turn and address your conversation to some one else.

It is very discourteous when a person begins to relate a circumstance or an anecdote, to stop them short by saying, "You have heard it before." Still worse to say you do not wish to hear it at all. There are people who set themselves against listening to anything that can possibly excite melancholy or painful feelings, and profess to hear nothing that may give them a sad or unpleasant sensation. Those who have so much tenderness for themselves have usually but little tenderness for others.

Generally speaking, it is injudicious for ladies to attempt arguing with gentlemen on political or financial topics. All the information that a woman can possibly acquire or remember on these subjects is so small in comparison with the knowledge of men that the discussion will not elevate them in the opinion of masculine minds. Still, it is well for a woman to desire enlightenment, that she may comprehend something of these discussions when she hears them from the other sex, but let her refrain from controversy and argument on such topics, as the grasp of the female mind is seldom capable of seizing or retaining. Men are very intolerant toward women who are prone to contradiction and contention when the talk is of things considered out of their sphere, but very indulgent toward a modest and attentive listener, who only asks questions for the sake of information. Men like to dispense knowledge; but few of them believe that, in departments exclusively their own, they can profit much by the suggestions of women.

In talking with a stranger, if the conversation should turn toward sectarian religion, inquire to what Church he belongs, and then mention your own Church. This, among people of good sense and good manners, and, we may add, of true piety, will preclude all danger of remarks being made on either side which may be painful to either party. In giving your opinion of a new book, a picture, or a piece of music, when conversing with an author, an artist, or a musician, say, modestly, that " so it appears *to you* "—that " it has given you pleasure," or the contrary. But do not positively or dogmatically assert that it is good or that it is bad. The person with whom you are talking is, in all probability, a far more competent judge than yourself; therefore listen attentively, and he may correct your opinion and set you right. If he fail to convince you, remain silent or change the subject.

In being asked your candid opinion of a person, be very cautious to whom you confide that opinion, for, if repeated as yours, it may lead to unpleasant consequences. It is only to an intimate and long-tried friend that you may safely entrust certain things that, if known, might produce mischief. The practice so prevalent with officious people of repeating to their friends whatever they hear to their disadvantage cannot be too severely condemned. True, no lady entitled to the name will wantonly lacerate the feelings and mortify the self-love of those whom she calls her friends by telling them what has been said about them by other friends.

Few persons are good talkers who are not extensive and

miscellaneous readers. You cannot attentively read the best authors without obtaining a great command of words, so that you can with ease and fluency clothe your ideas in appropriate language. You may probably find yourself in a company where no one is capable of appreciating good conversation, and where, to be understood, or, indeed, to keep them awake, you must talk down to the capacities of your hearers. You must manage this adroitly, or they may find you out and be offended. But if you choose to scatter pearls where wax beads would be equally valued, do not introduce quotations from the poets or references to books with which your hearers are unacquainted, lest they wonder what they mean.

If placed beside a lady so taciturn that no effort on your part can draw her out, or elicit more than a monosyllable, and that only at long intervals, you may safely conclude that there is nothing in her, and leave her to her own dulness or to be enlivened by the approach of one of the other sex.

OBLIGATIONS TO GENTLEMEN.

N her intercourse with gentlemen a lady should take care to avoid all pecuniary obligation. The civility which a gentleman conventionally owes to a lady is a sufficient tax—more she has no right to expect or accept. A man of good sense and of true politeness will not be offended at her unwillingness to become his debtor. On the contrary, he will respect her delicacy and approve her dignity, and consent at once to her becoming her own banker on all occasions where expense is to be incurred.

When invited to join a party to a place of amusement let her consent if she wishes ; but let her state expressly that it is only on condition of being permitted to pay for her own ticket. If she steadily adheres to this custom it will soon be understood that such is always her commendable practice ; and she can then, with perfect propriety, at any time ask for a seat among friends who intend going. To this accommodation she could not invite herself if in the continual habit of visiting public places at the expense of others. The best time for a lady to pay for herself is to put her money into the hand of the gentleman previous to their departure for the place of performance. He will not be so rude as to refuse it. If he does refuse, she should evince her resentment by going with him no more.

We disapprove of ladies going to charity fairs in the evening, when they require a male escort, and when that escort is likely to be drawn into paying exorbitant prices for gifts to his fair companion—particularly if induced to do so from the fear of appearing mean or of being thought wanting in benevolence. In the evening the young ladies who "have tables" are apt to become especially importunate in urging the sale of their goods, and appear to great disadvantage as amateur shop-keepers, exhibiting a boldness in teazing that no real shop-woman would presume to display. Then the crowd is generally great; the squeezing and pushing very uncomfortable; and most of the company far from genteel. Ladies who are ladies should only visit fancy fairs in the day-time, when they can go without gentlemen, none of whom take much pleasure in this mode of raising money, or rather of levying contributions for special purposes.

If you have occasion to send by a gentleman a parcel to a carrier's or railway office give him, along with it, the money to pay for its carriage. If you borrow change return it to him punctually. He ought to take it as a thing of course, without any comment. When you commission him to buy anything for you, if you know the price, give him the money before-hand; otherwise, pay it as soon as he brings the article.

When visiting a fancy shop with a gentleman, refrain from excessively admiring any handsome or expensive article you may chance to see there; above all, express no wish that you were able to buy it, and to regret that you cannot, lest he should construe these extreme tokens of admiration into hints that you wish him to buy it for you. To allow him to do so would, on your part, be very mean and indelicate, and on his very foolish.

It ought to be a very painful office for young ladies to go round soliciting from gentlemen subscriptions for charitable purposes. Still it is done. Subscription papers should only be offered by persons somewhat advanced in life and of undoubted respectability; and then the application should be made exclusively to those whose circumstances are known to be affluent. When you ask money for a charitable purpose, do so only when quite alone with the person to whom you apply. It is taking an undue advantage to make the request in the presence of others, particularly if there is not wealth as well as benevolence. There is a time for all things, and young ladies are deservedly unpopular when, even in the cause of charity, they seize every opportunity to levy contributions on the purses of gentlemen.

It is wrong to trouble gentlemen with commissions that may cause them inconvenience and expense. We repeat that a lady cannot be too particular in placing herself under obligations to a gentleman. She should scrupulously avoid it in every little thing that may involve him in expense on her account; and he will respect her the more.

BORROWING.

UY any article you are likely to want on more than one occasion rather than borrow. If your own, you can have it always at hand ; you will lay yourself under no obligation to a lender and incur no responsibility as to its safety while in your possession. But when you do borrow, see that the article is speedily returned. And under no consideration take the liberty of lending it to any person whatever before restoring it to the owner. Apologies and expressions of regret are no compensation, should it be out of your power to replace it if injured or lost.

No articles are more frequently borrowed than umbrellas, and none are returned with so little punctuality. Frequently a borrowed umbrella is never thought of by the borrower till after the weather clears up, the lender most probably suffering inconvenience for want of it. Often, it is detained till the next rain, when the lender has to take the trouble of sending for it. And then it is very possible it may not be found at all, some person in the mean time having nefariously carried it off. In such a case it is a matter of common honesty for the careless borrower to replace that umbrella with a new one, as she is not to suppose that empty expressions of regret or unmeaning apologies will be sufficient compensation for a substantial loss. When a friend lends you a handkerchief, a collar, or any other washable article, see that it is nicely washed and done up before returning it to her, and do so promptly. If an article of jewellery, carry it back to her yourself, and put it into her own hand, to preclude all risk of loss. She will not be so ungenerous as to tell any person that she has lent it to you, and will, for a while afterwards, refrain from wearing it herself in any company where it may be recognized.

On borrowing a book immediately put a cover upon it, and let the cover be of clean, smooth, white or light-coloured paper. What is called " nankeen " paper is best and strongest for this purpose. Make no remarks with pen or pencil on the margin of any book that does not belong to yourself. Whatever may be your opinion of certain passages, you have no right to disturb other readers by obtruding upon them opinions unasked for. In a book even belonging to yourself it is well to use the pencil sparingly, and only to correct an error of the press or a chronological mistake of the author. All readers like to form their own opinions as they go along, without any promptings from those who have preceded them.

Be particularly careful of borrowed magazines, as the loss of one number spoils a whole set, and you may have great difficulty in replacing a lost number. Even a newspaper should be punctually returned. The owner may wish to file it or to send it away to a friend. If lost or defaced while in your possession, send to the publishing office and buy another. It is unsafe to leave the book you are reading in the parlour of a hotel. Always carry it away with you whenever you quit the room—otherwise you will be likely to see it no more.

If, while in your possession, a borrowed book is irreparably

43

injured, it is your duty to replace it by purchasing for the owner another copy. And if that cannot be procured, all you can do is to buy a work of equal value and to present that, as the only compensation in your power. Observe the same rule with all borrowed articles lost or injured. The lender is surely not the person to suffer from the carelessness of the borrower.

By-the-by, in taking up a print to look at, always extend it carefully with both hands, that the paper may be in no danger of cracking or rumpling, which it cannot escape if held but in one hand, particularly if there is a breeze blowing near it. To show a large engraving without risk of injury, spread it out smoothly on a table, keeping it flat by means of books or other weights laid carefully down on the corners, and, if the plate is very large, at the sides also.

In borrowing a dress as a pattern, it is safest not to try it upon yourself lest some part of the body should be stretched or frayed. Also, in trying on a hat or cap that is not your own, see that it is not wrinkled or rumpled or soiled. Never put on another person's gloves.

Avoid borrowing change or small sums. It is possible that you may really forget to repay them; but then it is also possible that you may be suspected of forgetting wilfully. With regard to the practice of borrowing articles of household use, it is generally a custom " more honoured in the breach than the observance," particularly when living in a place where all such things can be easily obtained by sending to the shops. There are persons who, with ample means of providing themselves with all that is necessary for domestic service, are continually troubling their neighbours for the loan of this, that, or the other thing. If articles must be borrowed, let them be returned promptly, and in good order.

BORROWING.

If, in consequence of the unexpected arrival of company, anything for the table is borrowed, such as tea, coffee, &c., see that it is punctually returned, equal in quantity and in quality, or rather superior. Habitual borrowers are very apt to forget this piece of honesty, either neglecting to return the things at all or meanly substituting inferior articles.

PRESENTS.

HAVING accepted a present, it is your duty, and ought to be your pleasure to let the giver see that you make use of it, as intended, and that it is not thrown away upon you. If it is an article of dress or of personal decoration, take occasion, on the first suitable opportunity, to wear it in presence of the giver. If an ornament for the centre table or the mantelpiece, place it there. It a book, do not delay reading it. Afterwards, speak of it to her as favourably as you can. If of fruit or flowers, refer to them the next time you see her.

In all cases when a gift is sent to you return a note of thanks, or at least a verbal message to that effect.

PRESENTS.

Never inquire of the giver what was the price of her gift, or where she bought it. To do so is considered extremely rude.

When an article is presented to you for a specified purpose, it is your duty to use it for that purpose and for no other, according to the wish of the donor. It is mean and dishonourable to give away a present—at least without obtaining permission from the original giver. You have no right to be liberal and generous at the expense of another, or to accept a gift with a secret determination to bestow it yourself on somebody else. If it is an article that you do not want—that you possess already, or that you cannot use for yourself, it is best to say so candidly, at once expressing your thanks for the offer, and requesting your friend to keep it for some other person to whom it will be advantageous.

It is fit that the purchaser of the gift should have the pleasure of doing a kindness with her own hand, and eliciting the gratitude of one whom she knows herself.

Making a valuable present to a rich person is, in most cases, a work of supererogation, unless the gift is of something rare or unique, which cannot be purchased, and which may be seen and used to more advantage at the house of your friend than while in your possession. But to give an expensive article of dress, jewellery, or furniture to one whose means of buying such things are quite equal (if not superior) to your own, is an absurdity, though not a very uncommon one, as society is now constituted.

There are persons who, believing that presents are generally made with some mercenary view, and being unwilling themselves to receive favours or incur obligations, make a point of repaying them as soon as possible by a gift of something equivalent. This at once implies that they suspect the motive. If sincere in her friendship, the donor of the first present wil

47

feel hurt at being directly paid for it, and consider that she has been treated rudely and unjustly. On the other hand, if compensation was secretly desired and really expected, she will be disappointed at receiving nothing in return. Therefore, among persons who can conveniently provide themselves with whatever they may desire, the bestowal of presents is generally a most unthankful business. If you are in opulent circumstances it is best to limit your generosity to such friends only as do not abound in the gifts of fortune, and whose situation denies them the means of indulging their tastes. By them such acts of kindness will be duly appreciated and gratefully remembered ; and the article presented will have a double value if it is to them a novelty.

When a young lady of fortune is going to be married her friends are all expected to present her with bridal gifts. It is a custom that sometimes bears heavily on those whose condition allows them but little to spare. And from that little it may be very hard for them to squeeze out enough to purchase some superfluous ornament, or some article for a centre table, when it is already covered with the gifts of the wealthy—gifts lavished on one who is really in no need of such things, and whose marriage confers no benefit on any one but herself.

When the young couple have not an abundance of the "goods of this world," the case is different ; and it may then be an act of real kindness for the opulent friends of the bride to present her with any handsome article of dress or of furniture that they think will be acceptable. What we contend is, that on the occasion of a marriage in a wealthy family the making of presents should be confined to the immediate relatives of the lady, and only to such of them as can well afford it.

At christenings it is, fortunately, the sponsors only that are expected to make gifts to the infant. Therefore, invite no

48

persons as sponsors who cannot well afford this expense, unless you are sufficiently intimate to request them privately not to comply with the custom, being unwilling that they should cause themselves inconvenience by doing so.

The presentation of Christmas and New Year's gifts is often a severe tax on persons with whom money is not

plenty. It would be well if it were the universal custom to expect and receive no presents from any but the rich.

In making gifts to children choose for them only such things as will afford them somewhat of lasting amusement. For boys, kites, tops, balls, marbles, wheelbarrows, carts, gardening utensils, and carpenters' tools, &c. Showy toys that are merely to look at, and from which they can derive no enjoyment but in breaking them to pieces, are not worth buying. Little girls delight in small tea-sets and dinner-sets, in which they can "make feasts," miniature kitchen utensils to play at cooking, washing, &c., and dolls so dressed that all the clothes can be taken off and put on at pleasure.

Young ladies should be careful how they accept presents from gentlemen. No truly modest and dignified woman will incur such obligations. And no gentleman who really respects her will offer her anything more than a bouquet, a book, one or two autographs of distinguished persons, or a few relics or mementoes of memorable places—things that derive their chief value from associations. But to present a young lady with articles of jewellery, or of dress, or with a costly ornament, ought to be regarded as an offence rather than a compliment, excusable only in a man sadly ignorant of the refinements of society. And if he is so, she should set him right, and civilly, but firmly, refuse to be his debtor.

In presenting a dress to a friend whose circumstances are not so good as your own, and who you know will gladly receive it, select one of excellent quality, and of a colour that you think she will like. She will feel mortified if you give her one that is low-priced, flimsy, and of an unbecoming tint.

When you give a dress to a poor woman it is far better to buy for her a substantial new one than to bestow on her an old thin dress of your own. The poor have little time to sew for themselves, and second-hand fine clothes last them but a very short time before they are fit only for the rag-bag.

If you are going to have a party, and among your very ntimate friends is one whose circumstances will not permit her to incur the expense of buying a handsome new dress for the occasion, and if she has no choice but to stay away, or to appear in a costume very inferior to that of the other ladies, you may (if you can well afford it) obviate this difficulty by presenting her with a proper dress and other accessories. This may be managed anonymously, but it will be better to do it with her knowledge. It will be a very gratifying mark of your friendship; and she ought to consider it as such, and not to refuse it from a feeling of false pride. Of course it will be kept a secret from all but yourselves.

DEPORTMENT AT A HOTEL.

HERE there is so much travelling now in the summer (and, indeed, at all seasons) it may be useful to offer some hints on the propriety of manners which ought to be observed in places where you are always exposed to the inspection and to the remarks of strangers. These strangers, knowing you but slightly, or not at all, will naturally draw their inferences for or against you from what they see before their eyes, concluding that you are genteel or ungenteel, patrician or plebeian, according to the coarseness or the polish of your manners.

It is usual for members of the same party to meet in the ladies' drawing-room before they go in to breakfast, unless the party is large; and then it is not expected that half a dozen persons should be kept waiting for one or two late risers or tardy dressers. When one or two of the party find themselves ready in the parlour, it will be best for them to proceed to the breakfast-room, and leave the others to follow at their convenience by twos or by threes, always seeing that a young lady, if a stranger, is not left to go in alone. Strangers at hotels

52

can have no particular seats at breakfast and tea, as at these repasts they always come to table by instalments and at no regular time.

It is not genteel to go to the breakfast-table in any costume approaching to full dress. There must be no flowers or ribbons in the hair. A morning cap should be as simple as possible. The most genteel morning dress is a close gown of some plain material, with long sleeves, which, in summer, may be white muslin. A merino or cashmere wrapper (grey, brown, purple, or olive) faced or trimmed with other merino of an entirely different colour, such as crimson, scarlet, green, or blue, is a becoming morning dress for winter. In summer, a white cambric-muslin morning robe is the handsomest breakfast attire, but one of gingham or printed muslin the most convenient. The coloured dress may be made open in front with short, loose sleeves and a pointed body. Beneath it, a white under-dress, having a chemisette-front down to the belt, and long white sleeves down to the wrist. This forms a very graceful morning costume, the white skirt appearing where the coloured skirt opens.

The fashion of wearing black silk mittens at breakfast is now obsolete. It was always inconvenient, and neither useful nor ornamental.

It is usual at a hotel table for each waiter to have charge of three or four persons, and to attend to their wants exclusively. If you are a stranger, ask the waiter his name when he first comes to you; and, unless he is not at hand, and you see another standing idle, do not call on any one else to attend you. When speaking to the waiter, address him in a distinct, but not in too loud a voice, and always civilly. Thank him for any little extra attention he may show you. If you do not like what he has brought you, or find that you cannot eat it, make your objection in a low voice, so as not to be heard by the neighbouring guests, and quietly desire him to bring you something else.

After breakfast, it is customary for the ladies to adjourn to the drawing-room, where they converse or read the papers, or receive early visitors, while the chambermaids are putting the bed-chambers in order. Some who are not accustomed to hotels go immediately from the breakfast-table to their own apartment, sitting there among the flue and dust during the whole process of bed-making and room-sweeping, afraid to trust the chambermaid alone lest she should steal something. This is absurd. They should know that the chambermaids (being all considered honest and responsible) are furnished with duplicate keys, by which they can at any time unlock the chamber-doors and let themselves in when the occupant is absent. Also, this palpable suspicion of their honesty is an insult to the girls, and is always felt as such.

Should you perceive that the dress of another lady is, by some accident, out of order—for instance, that a hook or a button has become unfastened, or that a string is visibly hanging out, a collar unpinned and falling off, the corner of a shawl dragging along the floor, a skirt caught up, or a sleeve slipping down—immediately have the kindness to apprise her of it in a low voice, and assist her in repairing the mischance, and, if necessary, leave the room with her for that purpose.

Bring no large sewing into the ladies' drawing-room, and nothing that will produce clippings or litter. Whenever you have occasion to write more than a few lines, do it in your own apartment. It is well to have always there a small writing-case of your own, with paper, pens, ink, wafers, sealing-wax, envelopes, postage stamps, &c.

Except in cases of illness, it is well to decline invitations to visit ladies in their own apartments, unless you are very intimately acquainted with them or have some particular business. Too much sociability may induce communications too confidential ; .nd subsequent events may prove this confidence to be misplaced. Among the ladies staying at a hotel there is always more harmony when they all content themselves with meeting at table or in the public drawing-room.

There is no impropriety in a lady commencing a conversation with another lady or stranger of genteel appearance. But you should be previously certain of her respectability, more especially if she is travelling without a companion.

In a public parlour it is selfish and unmannerly to sit down to a piano uninvited and begin playing or practising without seeming to consider the probability of your interrupting or annoying the rest of the company, particularly when you see them all engaged in reading or in conversation. It is difficult to understand how a young stranger can walk up to the instrument, sometimes almost as soon as she arrives, and rattle over the keys, drowning the voices of ladies and gentlemen who may be talking, and therefore compelling them to cease their conversation. To read when piano-playing is going on is, to most persons, impossible. If the music is really very good, and accompanied by a fine voice, it is true that most readers will willingly close the book to listen. But if the playing is barely tolerable, or decidedly bad, and if the singing is weak and insipid, or harsh and screaming, or timeless, who can possibly wish to hear it ? No lady should play or sing in company unless she knows herself to be universally recognized a good singer or player, and capable of something more than the mere series of lessons she has learnt from her music eacher.

It is customary with professional or public musicians, when in private company, to volunteer a song or a piece, knowing that, out of delicacy, no one will ask them to give a gratuitous specimen of the art by which they live. This is polite and proper. It is always duly appreciated, and adds to the popularity of the performer.

In conversing with gentlemen at hotels (and all other places) try not to fall into the too common practice of talking to them nothing but nonsense. It is hard to understand that so many ladies of good abilities and cultivated minds, and who always, with their own sex, talk like intelligent, sensible, women, should, as soon as they get into conversation with a gentleman, give way at once to something they call excitement—now the fashionable word for every feeling that is wrong.

It is not to be supposed that there is any objection to that sprightliness which is one of the most agreeable characteristics of youth. On the contrary, one is glad to see vivacity in women of all ages ; and if they have a sprinkling of wit and humour, so much the better. But we wish them to do themselves justice, and not, when conversing with men, to say what is pointless, vapid, and insipid. We do not wish ladies, in conversing even with men of sense, to confine themselves always to grave discussions on important subjects. On the contrary, gay and lively conversation is always pleasant when well-timed ; but those who have not a talent for wit and humour had better not attempt it.

If you own a lap-dog or poodle, recollect that, however charming it may be to yourself, others may regard it as an annoyance ; therefore, try to do without it when you are in the parlour of a house that is not your own, and when the company present does not consist entirely of your own family.

If, while in the parlour of the hotel, you wish to know if a person you are desirous of seeing is staying at the house, the easiest way to obtain the information is not to inquire round of the ladies present, but to ring the bell and desire the waiter to make inquiries. You can then send a message accordingly. It should be a card, with a message pencilled on it.

If, when about to ascend the stairs, you find that a gentleman is going up at the same time, draw back and make a sign for him to precede you. He will bow and pass on before you. When coming down do the same, that the gentleman may descend in advance of you. A very polished man will not wait for a signal from the lady, but will bow and run up-stairs, passing her as a thing of course.

In ringing a bell one pull is sufficient, and always pull the cord downward. If you jerk it out horizontally and give successively several hard pulls in that direction, the chord is very likely to break, or the knob or tassel come off in your hand.

HOTEL DINNER.

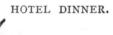

N dressing for a hotel dinner, it is not in good taste to adopt a full evening costume, and to appear as if attired for a ball; for instance, with a coloured velvet robe, or one of a splendid brocade, or a transparent gauze material over a satin, or with short sleeves and bare neck in cold weather, or with flowers or jewels in the hair. Such costumes should be reserved for evening parties. If worn at the *table d'hôte*, it may be suspected you have no other place in which to display them. Your dress need not be more showy than you would wear when dining at a private house. There is no place where dress escapes with less scrutiny than at a hotel. Still it is bad taste to go to the dinner table in ungenteel and unbecoming habiliments, such as a figured or party-coloured *mousseline-de-laine*, a thing which has always the effect of calico, and like calico gives an unladylike look even to the most decided lady.

A profusion of jewellery at a public table is in very bad taste, particularly if the jewellery is palpably false ; for instance—a brooch with mock diamonds, or a string of wax beads, meant for pearls, or glass things imitating topazes or garnets. A large imitation gem always betrays its real quality by its size.

Endeavour to make your arrangements so as to be dressed for dinner, and seated in the ladies' drawing-room about ten or fifteen minutes before the dining hour, that you may be ready to go in with the rest of the company.

In seating yourself, look down for a moment to see if you have placed the foot of your chair on the dress of the lady sitting next to you ; and, if you have done so, remove it instantly, that her dress may not be torn when she attempts to rise.

Sit close to the table, but never lean your elbows upon it. To sit far from it and reach forward is very awkward. Having unfolded your napkin, secure it to your belt with a pin to prevent its slipping down and falling under the table. This may be done so that the pinning will not be perceptible.

Refrain from loud talking or loud laughing. Young ladies are never conspicuously noisy at a dinner table or anywhere else. Still more carefully refrain from whispering or exchanging significant glances. Whispers are always overheard, and glances are always observed.

59

When eating fish, first remove the bones carefully and lay them on the edge of your plate, then with your fork in your right hand, and a small piece of bread in your left, take up the flakes of fish. Servants and all other persons should be taught that butter sauce should not be poured over the fish but put on one side of the plate, that the eater may use it profusely or sparingly according to taste, and be enabled to mix it conveniently with the sauce from the fish castors. Pouring butter sauce over anything is now ungenteel.

Do not attempt removing a cover from the dish that you may help yourself before the rest of the company. Leave all that to the waiters; tell them what you want in a distinct but not in a loud, conspicuous voice. Where servants are numerous, they should always go by their surnames, which will prevent the confusion arising from half a dozen Johns or as many Williams.

If the waiters are attentive, and in sufficient number, you will have, at a good hotel, little or no occasion to help yourself to anything. Do not under any circumstances reach across the table, or rise on your feet to get at any particular dish you may want. Trouble no one of the company; but wait till you see a servant at hand. If in turning to speak to a waiter you find him in the act of serving some one else say, "When you are at leisure I will thank you for some ——." It is selfish to be continually sending out of the room the man who waits near you for the purpose of bringing extra things for yourself; try to be satisfied with what you find on the table, and recollect that you are depriving others of his services while you are sending him back and forward on errands to the kitchen.

Many persons hold silver forks awkwardly as if not accustomed to them. It is fashionable to use your knife only while cutting up the food small enough to be eaten with the fork alone. While cutting keep your fork in your left hand, the hollow or concave side downward, the fork in a very slanting position, and your forefinger far down upon its handle. When you have done cutting up what you are going to eat lay aside your knife, transfer the fork to your right hand, and take a small piece of bread in your left. If eating anything soft, use your silver fork somewhat as a spoon, turning up the hollow side that the cavity may hold the food. If engaged in talking, do not meanwhile hold your fork bold upright, but incline it downward, so as to be nearly on a level with your plate. Remember always to keep your own knife, fork, and spoon out

of the dishes. It is an insult to the company, and a disgrace to yourself to dip into a dish anything that has been, even for a moment, in your mouth. To take butter or salt with your own knife is an abomination. It is nearly as bad to take a lump of sugar with your fingers.

In eating bread at dinner break off little bits, instead of putting the whole piece in your mouth and biting at it.

No lady looks worse than when gnawing a bone, even of game or poultry. Few ladies do it. In fact, nothing should be sucked or gnawed in public. Always pare apples and peaches, and crack no nuts with the teeth. In eating cherries put your half-closed hand before your mouth to receive the stones; then lay them on one side of your plate.

Do not eat incongruous and unsuitable things from the same plate, telling the waiter that "he need not change it, as it will do very well."

If a lady wish to eat lobster, let her request the waiter that attends her to extract a portion of it from the shell, and bring it to her on a clean plate, also to place a castor near her. Novices in lobster sometimes eat it simply with salt, or with vinegar only, or with black pepper. To prepare it according to the usual custom—cut up, very small, the pieces of lobster, and on another plate make the dressing. First, mash together some hard-boiled yoke of egg, and some of the red coral of the lobster, with a little salt and cayenne. Mix in, with a fork, mustard to your taste, and then a liberal allowance of salad oil, finishing with vinegar. Transfer the bits of lobster to the plate that has the dressing, and combine the whole with a fork. Lettuce salad is dressed in the same manner.

At a public table a lady should never volunteer to dress salad for others of the company. Neither should she cut up a pie and help it round. These things ought only to be done by a gentleman, or a servant.

If a gentleman with whom you are acquainted has dressed a salad, and offers the plate to you, take what you want, and immediately return to him the remainder, and do not pass it on to persons in your vicinity. It is his privilege and not yours to offer it to others, as he has had the trouble of dressing it. And it is just that he should have a portion of it for himself, which will not be the case if you officiously hand it about to people around you.

It was formerly considered ill-bred to refuse to take wine with a gentleman. Now it is no longer an offence to decline these invitations. If you have no conscientious scruples, and if you are acquainted with the gentleman, or have been introduced to him, you may comply with his civility; and when both glasses are filled, look at him, bow your head, and taste the wine.

If a stranger whom you do not know, and to whom you have had no introduction, takes the liberty of asking you to drink wine with him, refuse at once, positively and coldly, to prove that you consider it an unwarrantable freedom. And so it is.

If you are helped to anything whose appearance you do not like, or in which you are disappointed, when you taste it you of course, at a hotel table, are not obliged to eat it. Merely leave it on your plate, without audibly giving the reason, and then, in a low voice, desire the waiter to bring you something else. It is well, while at table, to avoid any discussion of the demerits of the dishes. On the other hand, you may praise them as much as you please.

In refusing to be helped to any particular thing, never give as a reason that, " You are afraid of it," or " that it will dis-agree with you." It is sufficient, simply to refuse, and then no one has a right to ask why. While at table all allusions to dyspepsia, indigestion, or any other disorders of the stomach, are vulgar and disgusting. The word stomach should never be uttered at any table, or, indeed, anywhere else, except to your physician, or in a private conversation with a female friend interested in your health. It is a disagreeable word (and so are all its associations), and should never be mentioned in public to " ears polite." Also make no remark on what is eaten by persons near you (except they are children, and under your care), such as its being unwholesome, indigestible, feverish, or in any way improper. It is no business of yours, and, besides, you are not to judge of others by yourself.

63

When the finger-glasses are sent round, dip a clean corner of the napkin into the water, and wet round your lips with it, but omit the singular foreign fashion of taking water into your mouth, rinsing and gurgling it round and then spitting it back into the glass. Wait till you can give your mouth a regular and efficient washing up-stairs. Dip your fingers into the glass, rub them with the slice of lemon that may be floating on the surface, and then wipe them on the napkin.

At hotels the interval between dinner and tea is usually short; the tea hour being early that the guests may have

ample time to prepare for going to places of amusement. Yet there are ladies who, though spending all the evening at home, will remain sitting idly in the parlour till eight o'clock, keeping the table standing and servants waiting in attendance. This is very inconsiderate. The servants certainly require rest, and should be exempt from all attendance in the ladies' room for an hour or two in the evening.

In making acquaintance with a stranger at a hotel, there is no impropriety (but quite the contrary) in inquiring of her

64

from what place she comes. In introducing yourself give your name audibly, or, what is better, if you have a card with you, present that, and she should do the same in return. Before you enter into conversation on any subject connected with religion it will be well to ask her to what Church she belongs. This knowledge will guard you from indulging inadvertently in sectarian remarks which may be displeasing to her, besides producing a controversy which may be carried too far.

When you give a gratuity to a servant—for instance, to the man who waits on you at table, or he that attends your room, or to the chambermaid or messenger—give it at no regular time, but whenever you think proper or find it convenient. It is injudicious to allow them to suppose that they are to do you no particular service without being immediately paid for it. It is, at the same time, right and customary to pay them extra for carrying your baggage up and down stairs when you are departing from the house or returning to it. If you are a permanent boarder, and, from ill-health, require extra attendance, it is well to give a certain sum monthly to each of the servants who wait upon you, and then they will not expect anything more except on extraordinary occasions.

All persons who go to hotels are not able to lavish large and frequent gratuities on the servants. But all, for the price they pay to the proprietor, are entitled to an ample share of attention from the domestics.

In all hotels it is against the rule to take out of the ladies' drawing-room any books that may be placed there for the general convenience of the company, such as dictionaries, guide-books, directories, magazines, &c. If you borrow a file of newspapers from the reading-room, get done with it as soon as you can, lest it should be wanted by others, and as soon as you have finished ring for a servant to carry the file back.

DEPORTMENT ON SHIPBOARD.

VERY one knows that there are few places where the looks and manners of the company are more minutely scanned than on shipboard, and few where the agreeability of a lady will be more highly appreciated. There is little or no variety of objects to attract attention. The passengers are brought so closely into contact with each other, and confined to so small a neighbourhood, or, rather, so many neighbours are crowded into so small a space, that all their sayings and doings are noticed with unusual attention by those who are well enough to regard anything but themselves. Sea-sickness is a very selfish malady, and no wonder that it is so.

It is best not to be over-officious in offering your aid to sick ladies, unless they are your intimate friends. The stewardess is generally all-sufficient, and much more capable of attending to their wants than you can be. Sea-sickness renders its victims very querulous, and few like to be continually reminded of their condition by inquiries too often repeated of—"How are you now?" "Do you feel any better?" or "Do you think you could eat something?" To one very much prostrated by the effects of the sea motion the mere replying to these questions is an additional misery.

If you are sick yourself, say as little about it as possible, and never allude to it at table, where you will receive but little sympathy, and, perhaps, render yourself offensive to all who hear you.

It is advisable for every lady on shipboard to endeavour to make herself as agreeable as she can, and not to suppose that all her "whims and oddities" will be excused because she is suffering "the pains and penalties of the sea." If free from sickness, a lady may propose or promote many pleasant little amusements and occupations, such as playing children's games on deck or taking a part in chess and backgammon in the cabin. Ladies sometimes form a regular little coterie, for assembling at certain hours and employing themselves in knitting, bead-work, and light sewing, &c., while a gentleman reads aloud to them. In the evening vocal concerts will be an agreeable change, as there are always some persons on board who can sing. And when the weather is fine and the ship steady a moonlight dance on deck is delightful.

Endeavour to live harmoniously with your fellow passengers. Avoid such national allusions as may give offence to any foreigners who may be on board. If you find that any of them are in the habit of sneering at your own country, or speaking of it disrespectfully, repress your resentment, resort to no recrimination, but refrain from further conversation with the person, and leave him to the gentlemen.

Avoid all argument with a woman of irritable disposition

lest you are drawn in yourself to defend your opinion **warmly.** You will soon find whether or not you can convince her, **or** whether she is likely to convince you. And it is worse than useless for both to continue protracting the argument when both know that the opinion of neither will be shaken. Long and turbulent discussions are particularly annoying on ship-board, particularly in rainy weather, when, for the weary and pent-up audience, "there is no door to cree out." Try to avoid supposing that every fresh gale is a violent storm, and confide in the excellence of the ship and the skill of its navigators. Yet, though not afraid yourself, remember that others may be so, and do not try to show your courage by indulging in undue gaiety. Mirth is out of place when the sky is overcast with gloom, the wind blowing hard, and the waves rising and foaming all round the vessel.

No captain likes to be teased with importunities concerning the probable length of the passage. You may be sure he will do all he can to make it as short as possible. In rough weather refrain from asking whenever you see him, "If there is any danger?" If there really is, he will certainly let you know it in time.

If you have, unfortunately, the rude and unamiable habit of laughing whenever you see any one get a fall, leave it off when on shipboard, where falls are of continual occurrence, from the rolling of the vessel and the steepness of the stairs. Low-bred women always say they cannot help laughing at such sights. We think ladies ought always to help it, and hasten at once to the relief of the sufferer to ascertain if any injury has been received.

A piano never sounds well on shipboard—the cabins are too small and the ceilings too low. To the sick and nervous this instrument is peculiarly annoying. You can practise when the weather is fine and the invalids are on deck. Pianos have been abolished in many of the best ships. Such instruments as can be carried on deck and played in the open air are, on the contrary, very delightful at sea when in the hands of good performers.

If there is any deficiency in accommodation or attentions, either endeavour, as well as you can, to do without them, or, in a kind and considerate manner, endeavour to obtain them from the servants, if not too inconvenient or against the ship's regulations.

OFFERS AND REFUSALS.

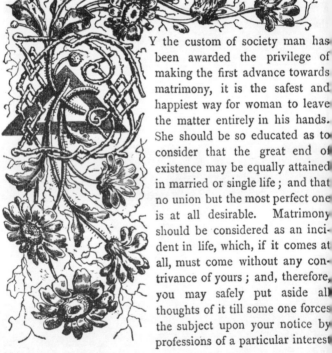

Y the custom of society man has been awarded the privilege of making the first advance towards matrimony, it is the safest and happiest way for woman to leave the matter entirely in his hands. She should be so educated as to consider that the great end of existence may be equally attained in married or single life; and that no union but the most perfect one is at all desirable. Matrimony should be considered as an incident in life, which, if it comes at all, must come without any contrivance of yours; and, therefore, you may safely put aside all thoughts of it till some one forces the subject upon your notice by professions of a particular interest in you.

Lively, ingenuous, conversable, charming girls often spoil into dull, bashful, silent young ladies, and all because their heads are full of nonsense about beaux and lovers. They have a thousand thoughts and feelings which they would be ashamed to confess, though not ashamed to entertain; and their preoccupation with a subject which they had better let entirely alone prevents their being the agreeable and rational companions of the gentlemen of their acquaintance, which they were designed to be.

Women are happily endowed with a sense of propriety and a natural modesty which will generally guide them aright in their intercourse with the other sex, and the more perfectly well-bred and discreet you are in your intercourse with female friends, the easier it will be for you to acquit yourself well with your male ones.

As soon as young ladies go into general society, they are liable to receive attentions that indicate a particular regard, and long before they are really old enough to form any such ties, often receive matrimonial overtures; it is, therefore, highly necessary to know how to treat them.

The offer of a man's heart and hand is the greatest compliment he can pay you, and, however undesirable to you those gifts may be, they should be courteously and kindly declined; and since a refusal is, to most men, not only a disappointment, but a mortification, it should always be prevented, if possible. Men have various ways of cherishing and declaring their attachment; those who indicate the bias of their feelings in many intelligible ways can generally be spared the pain of a refusal. If you do not mean to accept a gentleman who is paying you very marked attentions you should avoid receiving him whenever you can. You should not allow him to escort you; you should show your displeasure when joked about him; and if sounded by a mutual friend, let your want of reciprocal feelings be very apparent.

You may, however, be taken entirely by surprise, because there are men who are so secret in these matters that they do

not even let the object of their affections suspect their preference until they suddenly declare themselves lovers and
suitors. In such a case you will need all your presence of
mind, or the hesitation produced by surprise may give rise to
false hopes. If you have any doubt upon the matter, you
may fairly ask time to consider of it, on the grounds of your
never having thought of the gentleman in the light of a lover;
but if you are resolved against the suit, endeavour to make
your answer so decided as to finish the affair at once. Inexperienced girls sometimes feel so much the pain they are
inflicting that they use phrases which feed a lover's hopes; but
this is mistaken tenderness; your answer should be as decided
as it is courteous.

Whenever an offer is made in writing, you should reply to
it as soon as possible; and having in this case none of the
embarrassment of a personal interview, you can make such a
careful selection of words as will best convey your meaning.
If the person is estimable you should express your sense of
his merit and your gratitude for his preference in strong terms;
and put your refusal of his hand on the score of your not
feeling for him that peculiar preference necessary to the union
he seeks. This makes a refusal as little painful as possible,
and soothes the feelings you are obliged to wound. The
gentleman's letter should be returned in your reply, and your
lips should be closed upon the subject for ever afterwards.
It is his secret, and you have no right to tell it to any one;
but if your parents are your confidential friends, on all other
occasions he will not blame you for telling them.

Your young female friends should never be allowed to tease
or banter you into the betrayal of this secret. You cannot
turn your ingenuity to better account than by using it to baffle
their curiosity. Some girls are tempted to tell of an offer and
refusal in order to account for a cessation of those attentions

on the part of the gentleman which have before been so
constant and marked as to be observed by their friends.
But this is not a sufficient reason for telling another person's
secret.   You cannot always prevent a suspicion of the
truth, but you should never confirm it by any disclosure of
yours.

If you are so situated as to meet the gentleman whose
hand you have refused, you should do it with frank cordiality,
and put him at ease by behaving as if nothing particular had
passed between you. If this manner of yours is so far mistaken as to lead to a renewal of the offer, let him see as soon
as possible that he has nothing to hope from importunity, and
that if he would preserve your friendship he must seek for
nothing more.   Always endeavour to make true friends of
your rejected lovers by the delicacy and honour with which
you treat them.   If, when your own conduct has been unex-
ceptionable, your refusal to marry a man produces resentment,
it argues some fault of character in him, and can only be
lamented in silence.

Never think the less of a man because he has been refused,
even if it be by a lady whom you do not value highly.   It is
nothing to his disadvantage. In exercising their privilege of
making the first advances, the wisest will occasionally make
great mistakes, and the best will often be drawn into an affair
of this sort against their better judgment, and both are but
too happy if they escape with only the pain of being refused.
So far from its being any reason for not accepting a wise and
good man when he offers himself to you, it should only
increase your thankfulness to the Power which reserved him
for you, and to the lady through whose instrumentality he is
still free to choose.

DISAPPOINTED AFFECTIONS.

NE of the greatest trials in life to a woman is disappointment in love, either from an unrequited attachment or a misplaced one. It is the secret source of half the wretchedness and ill health that we see among women; and to guard sedulously against it should be one of the aims of female education, and the concern of the best friends of youth.

So very common is it for women to be disappointed in their first loves, that it has been said she considered the loss and recovery of the heart to be to the mind what the whooping cough or measles is to the body—a necessary disorder to be gone through, after which come maturity and health. But although we would not have our fair daughters to consider this painful experience of the heart as so inevitable a process, it is well to regard it as one from which it is possible entirely to recover. Religion has a balm for the heart's worst wounds. It has always been considered as a refuge for the unhappy.

but its power will be more perfectly manifested when the young and the gay embrace it, as the surest defence against sentimental suffering and the best guide to happiness in this world.

Love in the heart of a woman should partake largely of the nature of gratitude ; she should love, because she is already loved by one deserving her regard ; and, if she never allowed herself to think of gentlemen in the light of lovers or husbands until asked to do so, she would escape much suffering.

The credulity of women on the subject of being loved is very great. They often mistake a common liking for a particular regard, and on this foundation build up a castle in the air and fill it with all the treasures of their bright hopes and confiding love, and, when some startling fact destroys the vision, they feel as if the whole creation were a blank to them, and they were the most injured of women. It is safer to be very sceptical on the subject of being loved ; but if you do make the mistake, take all the blame to yourself and save your dignity by secrecy, if you cannot keep your heart from loving.

If you have only a wholesome dread of being entangled, and watch over your preferences with a jealous eye, you need never be caught in the snares of Cupid. If one person is becoming uppermost in your thoughts, if his society is more and more necessary to your happiness, if what he does and says seems more important than that of any one else, it is time to be on your guard, time to deny yourself the dangerous pleasure of his company, and indeed time to turn your thoughts resolutely to something else. The beginning o a preference may be checked ; it is only by indulgence that it becomes unmanageable. Speaking of it to any one, even to your bosom friend, is dangerous. So long as no one knows your weakness you have strong inducements to behave as if it did not exist, and that self-command is good for you. Directing the mind vigorously to some new study is a wholesome remedy, and a generous devotion of yourself to the interests and happiness of others will save you from dangerous reverie and painful reflection. There are few partialities which, if taken early enough and dealt with in this way, cannot be overcome without any breaking of hearts or destruction of health and happiness, whilst the power gained by such self-discipline is a permanent advantage to the character.

Where the attachment has ever been reciprocal, and has been allowed to gain ground before the necessity came for combating it, the struggle will, of course, be harder, and the suffering much greater. For this there is no sufficient remedy but vital piety, that giving up the heart to its Maker, which enables the Christian to say, "Whom have I in heaven but Thee, and there is none on earth that I desire besides Thee."

The cure for a wounded heart which piety affords is so complete that it makes it possible for the tenderest and most constant natures to love again. When a character is thus disciplined and matured, its sympathies will be called forth only by superior minds ; and if a kindred spirit presents itself as a partner for life, and is accepted, the union is likely to be such as will make the lady rejoice that her former predilection was over-ruled.

CORRESPONDENCE.

MUCH time is wasted, particularly by young ladies, in writing and answering such epistles as are termed "letters of friendship"—meaning long documents filled with regrets at absence, asseverations of affection, modest deprecations of self, and flattering references to the correspondent, or else anticipations of what may be coming and lamentations of what may be past, which are of no manner of use but to foster a sickly, morbid feeling, to encourage nonsense, and destroy a relish for such true friendship as is good and wholesome.

A still worse species of voluminous female correspondence is that which turns entirely upon love, or rather on what are called "beaux," or entirely on hate—for instance, hatred of stepmothers. This topic is considered the more piquant from its impropriety, and from its being carried on in secret.

77

Then there are young ladies born with the organ of letter-writing amazingly developed and increased by habitual practice, who can scarcely become acquainted with a gentleman possessing brains without volunteering a correspondence with him. And then ensues a long epistolary dialogue about nothing, or, at least, nothing worth reading or remembering; trenching closely on gallantry, but still not quite that; affected flippancy on the part of the lady, and an unaffected impertinence on that of the gentleman, alternating with pretended poutings on her side and half or whole laughing apologies on his. Sometimes there are attempts at moralizing or criticizing, or sentimentalizing—but nothing is ever elicited that, to a third person, can afford the least amusement or improvement, or excite the least interest.

No young lady ever engages in a correspondence with a gentleman who is neither her relative nor her betrothed without eventually lessening herself in his eyes. Of this she may rest assured. With some men it is even dangerous for a lady to write a note on the commonest subject. He may show the superscription, or the signature, or both, to his idle friends, and make insinuations much to her disadvantage, which his comrades will be sure to circulate and exaggerate.

Above all, let no lady correspond with a married man, unless she is obliged to consult him on business, and from that plain, straightforward path let her not diverge. Even if the wife sees and reads every letter, she will, in all probability, feel a touch of jealousy (or more than a touch) if she finds that they excite interest in her husband, or give him pleasure. This will inevitably be the case if the married lady is inferior in intellect to the single one, and has a lurking consciousness that she is so.

Having hinted what the correspondence of young ladies ought *not* to be, we will try to convey some idea of what it ought. Let us premise that there is no danger of any errors in grammar or spelling, and but few faults of punctuation, and that the fair writers are aware that a sentence should always conclude with a period, or full stop, to be followed by a capital letter beginning the next sentence, and that a new paragraph should be allotted to every change of subject, provided that there is room on the sheet of paper. And still it is well to have always at hand a dictionary and a grammar, in case of unaccountable lapses of memory. However, persons who have read much, and read to advantage, generally find themselves at no loss in orthography, grammar, and punctuation. To spell badly is disgraceful to a lady or gentleman, and it looks as if they had finished reading as soon as they left school.

The wording of your letter should be as much like conversation as possible, containing, in a condensed form, just what you would be most likely to talk about if you saw your friend. A letter is of no use unless it conveys some information, excites some interest, or affords some improvement. It may be handsomely written, correct in spelling, punctuation, and grammar, and yet stiff and formal in style—affectedly didactic, and, therefore, tiresome—or mawkishly sentimental, and, therefore, foolish. It may be refined and high-flown in words, but flat and barren in ideas, containing nothing that a correspondent cares to know.

Inexperienced letter-writers often feel provoked with themselves when they have filled a sheet without touching upon some topics that they fully intended to introduce, and perceive they have spread out one of inferior importance over half their paper. This may be avoided by considering before you begin all that you wish to write about, and allowing to each topic its proper space.

If your correspondent requires that her letters be kept

79

private from all friends, make it a point of honour to comply with her wishes, only make an exception in favour of your mother, in case she should desire to see the correspondence, for young ladies should gracefully acknowledge their parents' right of inspection; though, where there is a proper confidence on both sides, it will rarely be enforced.

The more rational and elevating the topics are on which you write, the less will you care for your letters being seen, or for paragraphs being read out of them, and where there is no need of any secrecy it is best not to bind your friend by promises, but to leave it to her discretion.

Do not feel bound to write to every one who begs you to do so, but choose carefully whom you will have in that relation, and when you have a few choice correspondents do not neglect them, and begin every letter with an apology, but write in due season, and waste no paper on commonplace excuses.

Madame de Sevigné praises her daughter for her attention to dates, which, she says, shows an interest in the correspondence; a dateless letter certainly loses much of its value, and they are but too common.

Remember the liability of a letter to miscarry, to be opened by the wrong person, to be seen by other eyes than those for whom it is meant, and be very careful what you write to the disadvantage of any one. Praise and admire, but beware of blame. Your judgment may be wrong, and you know not when nor where it may come up against you and make you sorry you ever penned it.

As you finish each page of your letter read it over to see that there are no errors. If you find any, correct them carefully. In writing a familiar letter, a very common fault is tautology, or a too frequent repetition of the same word—for instance, "Yesterday I received a letter from my sister Mary, which was the first letter I have received from my sister since she left." The sentence should be, "Yesterday I received a letter from my sister Mary, the first since she left us."

Unless you are writing to one of your own family, put always the pronoun "my" before the words "sister," "father," "mother," and not without it, as if they were also the relatives of your correspondent.

To end a sentence with the word "left" (for departed) is awkward and unsatisfactory—for instance, "It is two days since he left." Left what? It is one of the absurd innovations that have crept in among us of late years, and are supposed to be fashionable.

Avoid in writing, as in talking, all words that do not express the true meaning. Unless you know that your correspondent is well versed in French, refrain from interlarding your letters with Gallic words or phrases.

Do not introduce long quotations from poetry. Three or four lines of verse are sufficient; one line or two are better still. Write them rather smaller than your usual hand, and leave a space at the beginning and end, marking their commencement and termination with inverted commas, thus " ".

Unless to persons living in the same house, do not enclose one letter to another. And even then it is not always safe to do so. Let each letter be transmitted on its own account by mail, with its own full direction and its own postage-stamp. Confide to no one the delivery of an important letter intended for another person.

To break the seal of a letter directed to another person is punishable by law. To read secretly the letter of another is morally as felonious. A woman who would act thus meanly is worse than those who apply their eyes or ears to key-holes or door-cracks, or who listen under windows, or who, in a dusky parlour, before the lamps are lighted, ensconce themselves in a corner, and give no note of their presence while listening to a conversation not intended for them to hear.

We do not conceive that, unless he authorizes her to do so (which he had best not), a wife has a right to open her husband's letter, or he to read hers. Neither wife nor husband has any right to entrust to the other the secrets of their friends ; and letters may contain such secrets. Unless under extraordinary circumstances, parents should not consider themselves privileged to inspect the correspondence of grown-up children. Brothers and sisters always take care that their epistles shall not be unceremoniously opened by each other. In short, a letter is the property of the person to whom it is addressed, and nobody has a right to read it without permission. If you are shown an autograph signature at the bottom of a letter, be satisfied to look at that only, and do not open out and read the whole, unless desired.

The letters of a regular correspondent should be endorsed and filed as regularly by young ladies as by merchants ; this facilitates your reference to any one of them, prevents their being lost or mislaid, or exposed to curious eyes, saves your table from being strewed, and your letter-case from being crowded with them.

The letters of past years should either be destroyed or carefully locked up, with directions on the box that in case of your death they are to be returned unread to the writers, or, if that cannot be done, that they should be burnt unread. This disposal of letters after death is often the only important part of a young girl's last wishes, and yet it is rarely provided for. It is best to be always so prepared by making the necessary arrangements whilst in health.

The letters of very young persons rarely have any interest beyond the period in which they are written ; they are very seldom read after they are a year old ; and the idea of keeping them for future perusal is altogether chimerical. Life is too much crowded with novel interests to allow time for reading over quires of paper filled with the chat of young girls, however good it may have been in its day ; and, therefore, the wisest plan is to agree with your correspondent to make each a bonfire of the other's letters when they shall be more than a year old. A year's letters are enough for a memorial of your friend, if she be taken from you ; and by keeping the latest you will have her most mature compositions.

Notes of invitation should always designate both the day of the week and that of the month. If that of the month only is specified, one figure may, perhaps, be mistaken for another ; for instance, the 13th may look like the 18th, or the 25th like the 26th. We know instances where, from this cause, some of the guests did not come till the day after the party.

There are some very sensible people who, in their invitations, tell frankly what is to be expected ; and if they really ask but a *few* friends, they at once give the names of those friends, so that you may know who you are to see. If you are to meet no more than can sit round the tea-table they signify the same. If they expect twenty, thirty, or forty persons they say so, and do not leave you in doubt whether to dress for something very like a party, or for a mere family tea-drinking.

If it is a decided music party by all means specify the same, that those who have no enjoyment of what is considered fashionable music may stay away.

Always reply to a note of invitation the day after you have received it. To a note on business send an answer the same day. After accepting an invitation, should anything occur to prevent your going, send a second note in due time.

6—2

Do not take offence at a friend because she does not invite you every time she has company. Her regard for you may be as warm as ever, but it is probably inconvenient for her to have more than a certain number at a time. Believe that the omission is no evidence of neglect, or of a desire to offend you ; but rest assured that you are to be invited on other occasions. If you are not, then indeed you may take it as a hint that she is no longer desirous of continuing the acquaintance. Be dignified enough not to call her to account; but cease visiting her without taking her to task and bringing on a quarrel. But if you must quarrel let it not be in writing. A paper war is always carried too far, and produces bitterness of feeling, which is seldom, if ever, entirely eradicated, even after apologies have been made and accepted. Still, when an offence has been given in writing, the atonement should be made in writing also.

Avoid giving letters of introduction to people whose acquaintance cannot possibly afford any pleasure or advantage to those whose civilities are desired for them, or who have not leisure to attend to strangers. Professional people, to whom " time is money," and whose income stops whenever their hands and eyes are unemployed, are peculiarly annoyed by the frequency of introductory letters brought by people with whom they can feel no congeniality, and whom they never would have sought for. Many men of worth are not in a situation to entertain strangers handsomely, which means expensively. They may be kept in straitened circumstances through a thousand causes, and therefore unable to bear incessant demands on their time, attention, and purse. And in numerous instances letters are asked and given with no better motive than the gratification of idle curiosity.

Bores are particularly addicted to asking letters of introduction in accordance with their system of bestowing their tediousness upon as many people as possible. The kind friends from whom these missives are required are to be pitied, as they appear to have not the courage to refuse, or address enough to excuse themselves plausibly from complying.

In obtaining an introductory letter to a public favourite, say to a painter, for instance, ascertain before presenting it what branch of the art he professes. Also, no one should presume to request an introduction to an authoress if they are ignorant whether she writes prose or verse. Not that they are expected to talk to her immediately on literary subjects. Far from it. But if they know nothing of her works they deserve no letter. Letters of introduction should not be sealed. To do so is rude and mean. If you wish to write on the same day to the same person take another sheet, write as long an epistle as you please, seal it, and send it by mail.

It is best to deliver an introductory letter in person, as the lady or gentleman whose civilities have been requested in your behalf may thus be spared the trouble of calling at your lodgings, with the risk of not finding you at home. This is very likely to happen if you send instead of taking the letter yourself. If you do send it, enclose a card with your address upon it. Also, it is more respectful to go yourself than to expect them to come to you.

As soon as you are shown into the parlour send up the etters, and wait till the receiver comes to you.

When a letter is brought to you by a private hand, the usual ceremony is to defer reading it till the bringer has departed, unless he desires you to read it at once, which he will, if it is evidently a short letter. If a long one, request him to excuse you a moment, while you look at the beginning to see if your correspondent is well.

On farewell cards it is usual to write with a pencil the letters

"T. T. L.," "to take leave;" or "P. P. C.," "*pour prendre congé;*" or "P. D. A.," "*pour dire adieu*," "to bid adieu." In writing upon business exclusively your own, for instance, to make a request, to ask for information, to petition for a favour, or to solicit an autograph, it is but right not only to pay the postage of your own letter, but to enclose a stamp for the answer. This is always done by really polite and considerate people. You have no right, when the benefit is entirely your own, to cause any extra expense to the receiver of the letter, not even the cost of the postage back again. Also, in corresponding with a relation, or very intimate friend, to whom even a small expense is of more importance than to yourself, you may enclose a stamp for the answer. Do so always in writing to poor people.

COURTSHIP.

VERY young lady, especially on her first entrance into society, should be on her guard not to mistake the nature of the attentions she may receive. She will find men polite, assiduous, complimentary, admiring, and paying all those flatteries, both of words and actions, that are so agreeable, and to the inexperienced so seductive. Accept them all as your right, quietly and calmly, but never seem to give them more weight than in nine cases in ten they have. They are agreeable attentions which every gentleman is expected to pay, and every lady to receive. If not at first, a little experience will render you able to distinguish between the incense of the imagination and the earnest adoration of the heart. When this truth comes to you receive it truly ; truthfully accept it or frankly and kindly reject. Be in no hurry to have it thought that you have caught an admirer ; hurry no courtship into an engagement, make no engagement from which you cannot honourably withdraw at the first prompting of your heart; and never stand up to be married except to a man who is not only worthy of your deepest love, but whom you actually love with an entire devotion.

This love is an element of your own being. You love for yourself, and if you marry, it is the destiny, happy or miserable, of your own life. Do not marry for others. No human being has the right to violate any true instinct of your woman's heart, or put a constraint upon your love. This is written for those who have hearts, and who are capable of loving. But it is well not to mistake a caprice, a fancy, a romantic day-dream, the reflection of some want for a great and true passion. First love is never last love, unless the soul is crushed under some despotism. A whole series of light fancies, which might have been mistaken for love, have often been followed by the earnest passion of a life. These fancies float across the romantic mind of a young girl, like clouds across the summer sky—beautiful, but fleeting. Yet such a girl may wake from these dreams some day to the reality of a great love.

It is the custom for man to choose ; to propose ; to take the initiative in all tender proceedings ; and women have been educated to dress well, look pretty, and acquire accomplishments, and with a demure and modest reserve wait to be chosen. But the progress of the age now assigns to woman a nobler position. She is recognized as the queen of society—the sovereign of the empire of love. She has now far more to say and do than this pretty *rôle* would give her. The fashionable lady, in nine cases in ten, looks over the field, makes her choice from the circle of her admirers, gives the needed encouragement, and decides for herself her life's destiny. She may not absolutely make love to a man, but she chooses none the less, from those who are attracted to her, who shall make love to her. She does not actually propose, perhaps, but it is she who gives her chosen one the encouragement and permission to propose.

Before, however, you admit the attentions of a gentleman who wishes to pay you his addresses, very carefully examine your respective tastes and dispositions, and endeavour to settle in your own mind what are the most important requisites of happiness in the married state.

If a gentleman gives you reason to believe that he wishes to engage your affections, seek the advice of your parents, that

they may gain for you every necessary particular with regard to his morals and disposition, and means of suitably providing for you. If, unhappily, death has deprived you of parents, ask counsel of some one who will care for you, and on whose friendship you can rely. If you encourage the addresses of a deserving man, behave honourably and sensibly. Do not lead him about as if in triumph, nor take advantage of the ascendency which you have gained by playing with his feelings. Do not seek for occasions to tease him, that you may try his temper ; neither affect indifference or provoke lovers' quarrels, for the foolish pleasure of reconciliation. On your conduct during courtship will very much depend the estimation in which you will be held by your husband in after life.

Let neither rank nor fortune, nor the finest order of intellect, nor yet the most winning manners, induce you to accept the addresses of an irreligious man. Supposing your admirer be a man of sense, he will like religion in you, for your own sake ; if, on the contrary, such is not the case, and you become his wife, he will often, though perhaps without intention, distress you by his remarks ; and, it may be, regard with indifference your endeavours to form the minds of your children to virtue and piety.

It is as well to remember also that no happiness can be expected in the marriage state unless the husband is worthy of respect. Do not marry a weak man ; he is often intractable and capricious, and seldom listens to the voice of reason ; and most painful must it be to a woman to have to blush for her husband, and feel uneasy every time he opens his lips.

Every man with a nice sense of honour will indicate, by his prevailing bearing and language towards women, a *felt* distinction between the intentions of friendship and those of a suitor or lover. And while he observes towards all women and under all circumstances, the respectful courtesy due to them, he will not hesitate to make his purpose intelligible where he has conceived sufficient esteem to engender matrimonial intentions. Proper self-respect, as well as the consideration due to a lady and her friends, demands this.

No degree of devotion to one excuses incivility to other female acquaintances on the part of your admirer, and the most acceptable attentions to a woman of sense and delicacy are not those that render her generally conspicuous, but such as express an ever-present remembrance of her comfort, and a quick discernment of her real feelings and wishes.

So, in the matter of presents and similar expressions of politeness, good taste will dictate to your admirer; no lavish expenditure, unwarranted by pecuniary resources, and inconsistent with the general surroundings of either party, but rather a prevailing harmony that will be really a juster tribute to you of his regard, as well as a more creditable proof of his own tact and judgment. It is said that women judge of character by details; certain it is, that what may seem trifles often sensibly influence their opinions of men.

MARRIAGE.

OU should bear in mind that nothing in this life is of more importance for a woman to take a practical view of than marriage, nothing in which she should be more carefully guided by reason and good sense, and nothing, unfortunately, in which she is so much influenced by feeling, impulse, even accident. She will often spend more anxious thought, take more solicitous care in the choice of her house and the selection of its furniture than in studying the disposition and ascertaining the habits of him who is to be its master. "None are so blind as those who will not see," and of the multitudes of improvident and ill-assorted marriages that occur daily, there are very few that do not owe all their misery to simple rashness. The woman is wise who has the courage and prudence to weigh in time the different degrees of suffering, in disappointing and misplaced affections; when for the momentary gratification of a love that cannot last, she heaps up for herself a life-long repentance; or prepares for herself the temptation to do even worse, in severing by

93

divorce those ties God has declared shall never, but for one cause, be broken.

Women in this matter have no choice but that of accepting or rejecting offers made to them, but to compensate for this they have far greater powers of adaptation than men have. They can more easily conform themselves to circumstances and to the characters of their husbands than the husband can adapt his to his wife's.

We call this a compensation for the want of choice they have, and so it is, but it makes a wife's responsibilities greater, for she is the more to blame for estrangement if either, after marriage, finds the disposition and tastes of the other different from what was expected. Any close observer will perceive that the happiest and most united marriages are not

94

those where there is the greatest similarity of disposition, but those where, while each character has some traits in which the other is lacking, the wife has the good sense to put in practice this faculty of adapting herself to her husband's peculiarities of mind and taste.

Precisely because a wife's greatest claim on her husband is for submission, and just in proportion as each in little things, even more than great, understand and fulfil these duties, will their marriage be a united and happy one. Self-sacrifice is the truest womanly virtue, and above all in a wife ; not, as some do, by ostentatiously making martyrs of themselves, but in this loving, unobtrusive adaptation of herself to her husband's tastes and wishes. Unless singularly unfortunate in the husband she has found, such conduct as this will be the best security for some degree of happiness in marriages where the wife finds herself mistaken in her expectations.

"Well begun is half done" is remarkably true of marriage. The management of the first few months, after the novelty of their new life has a little worn off, but especially management on the wife's side, will probably give the tone to their whole ensuing life. An error at that time, the first discordance of wills, the first manifestation of difference of tastes and dispositions, will be—

> "The little rift within the lute
> That by-and-by will make all music mute,
> And, ever widening, slowly silence all."

Let the young wife beware, then, of making this "little rift" by even the shadow of a first quarrel. Quarrels are evil weeds that cannot be extirpated ; each one leaves a seed that will in time spring up and produce a plant stronger and more deeply rooted than the last.

A perfect marriage is so beautiful that God Himself chose

it as the type of the holiest, the closest of all unions, that between Himself and His Church; and, by the mouth of the Apostle, He holds up this union as an example of the reverence a wife should have for her husband. A true wife's affection and respect will ennoble her husband in her eyes, even if he is mentally her inferior; and where he is the superior her efforts to be worthy of him will ennoble her. When a husband has great and lofty aims in the world, no sympathy, no encouragement he can meet, will so support and cheer him as that of an earnest, true-hearted wife.

It is said there is a growing tendency among married women of education to hold maternal duties as onerous, to be unwilling to take the responsibilities and endure the trials and cares of maternity. The young lady who thinks of entering on matrimony without also seriously considering what her duties will be in this relation, and whether or not she will have the courage, patience, and tenderness to fulfil them,

" commits a folly and a crime." A large part of the duties of married life consists in the care of children, and the burden must be borne mostly by the mother. Very selfish and ungenerous is the woman's heart that is fain coldly to reject this most beautiful and holy of her duties, and, if forced to do so, reluctantly takes up, as a hard cross, what was intended should be for her, if faithful, rather a crown of honour and rejoicing. Bishop Dupanloup makes it one of his strongest arguments for mental cultivation in young ladies, and its persevering continuance after marriage, that they are bound to become in their earlier years the instructor, and, later, the guide and example of their children. He says, in substance, " ladies cannot be real companions and helpmates to their husbands—they cannot bear the part which they ought to bear in the education of their children—without this kind of interest and cultivation in themselves."

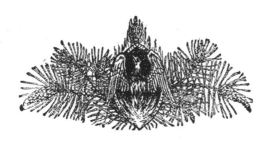

BRIDAL ETIQUETTE.

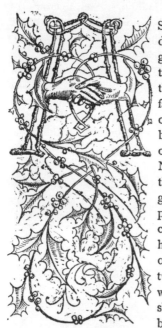

SSUMING that the important day is fixed, and that the bidden guests have accepted the invitation, the grand preoccupation of the female part of the lady's family is to prepare the bridal outfit or trousseau, which must be in accordance with the circumstances of the bride's family. Nevertheless, as it is an expense that few mothers grudge, they generally take an affectionate pride in rendering the outfit as complete as possible. We have heard of outfits in the class of wealthy merchants comprising twelve dozen chemises, trimmed with lace, a large assortment of slips, trimmed with embroidered bands, others plainer for morning use, an endless abundance of elegant night-caps, and countless pairs of stockings, from the silk hose and the gossamer-like open-work stockings down to the solid stocking for a country ramble. Dressing-gowns, muslin and silk dresses, and mantillas, should also be comprised in the outfit, as well as several bonnets, or hats, and suitable wrappings for winter.

Those who cannot afford such luxuries must substitute fewer articles of a more modest and durable kind. Such a stock is an invaluable groundwork to start with, and by supplying gradually each article as it wears out, the lady's wardrobe can be renewed without great expense.

Bridal Gifts.—Jewels are not comprised in an outfit. These should be presented by the bridegroom. Still, in families where there are family jewels, the daughter may have a portion set for her, according to the fashion of the day, over and above what her future husband may offer. Such, however, are exceptional cases. In less wealthy classes the husband would offer trinkets according to his means. Besides the latter, a watch, fan, a smelling-bottle, or any elegant article for the toilet or boudoir table, such as an ornamental candlestick, a desk of inlaid wood, or a fanciful standish, would be appropriate gifts. Any good old lace which the elders among the bride's female relations may happen to have amongst their stores is a most welcome present on such an occasion ; but if no aunts or other relations volunteer anything of the kind, the bride's mother should then supply the want, if she can afford it, or, in default of real lace, that pretty substitute, Irish point. A dress of black lace, and another of white lace, whether real or imitation, would likewise be a most useful addition to a trousseau, as well as feathers, ribbons, and any of those articles that can scarcely go out of fashion, and form an excellent *fonds-de-toilette*. But if the donors of bridal gifts really wish to benefit a bride not in affluent circumstances, we would suggest that they hold council together, so as not to double any superfluous article.

Bridesmaids.—A bride may have one or six bridesmaids at her choice. No particular number being fixed, it is often determined by the number of sisters, or of intimate friends, she may have. The bridesmaids should be dressed in white,

7—2

and all alike, and may wear orange-flower bouquets; they should avoid dressing like brides, which is out of place.

The Ceremony.—The bride uniformly goes to church in the same carriage with her parents, or with those who stand in their place; as, for instance, if the father is deceased, an elder brother or uncle, or even guardian, accompanies her mother and herself. If unhappily she is an orphan, and has no relations, a middle-aged lady and gentleman, friends of her parents, should be requested to take their place. A bridesmaid will also occupy a seat in the same carriage.

The bridegroom finds his way to church in a separate carriage, with his friends, or on foot, as the case may be; and he will show his gallantry by handing the bride from her carriage, and paying every attention to those who accompany her. Any omission in this respect cannot be too carefully avoided.

When before the altar, the father of the bride, or, in default of such relation, the nearest connection or some old friend, gives away the bride. The bridesmaids stand near the bride; and either her sister or some favourite friend will hold the gloves or handkerchief, as may be required, when she ungloves her hand for the wedding ring. When the ceremony is completed, and the names of the bride and bridegroom are signed in the vestry, they first leave the church together, occupying, by themselves, the carriage that waits to convey them to the house of the bride's father, or that of the guardian or friend by whom the bridal breakfast is given.

Bridal Breakfast.—The wedding cake uniformly occupies the centre of the table. It is often tastefully surrounded with flowers, among which those of the orange are conspicuous. After being cut according to the usages observed on such occasions, the oldest friend of the family proposes the lady's health; that of the bridegroom is generally proposed by some friend of his own, if present, but, if not so, by his father-in-law, or any of his new relatives, who will deem it incumbent upon them to say something gratifying to him while proposing his health, which courtesy he must acknowledge as best he can. The bride will retain her bridal costume during the breakfast. She occupies, with her husband, the centre of the table, and sits by his side—her father and mother taking the top and bottom, and showing all honour to the guests. When every compliment and kind wish has been proffered and acknowledged, the bride, attended by her friends, withdraws and exchanges her bridal costume for a walking-dress, before she starts for her wedding tour. Good taste points out that all bridal attributes should now be entirely discarded. Peculiarities that pertain to past days should be guarded against; mysteries concerning knives, forks, and plates, or throwing "an old shoe" after the bride, have long been exploded.

WEDDING CARDS.

MARRIAGE is usually announced in the newspapers, but, over and above, cards of the gentleman and lady, tied together with a silver cord, are sent round to the friends of each. The cards, which are furnished by the bridegroom, are twofold—one having the lady's name upon it, and the other the gentleman's. The envelope in which is placed the lady's card has her maiden name engraved inside the fold. In some circles it is customary to send cards almost immediately to friends and relations, mentioning at what time and hour the newly-married people expect to be called upon. When the newly-made pair contemplate a prolonged wedding trip no intimation is given on the cards of the day on which they will receive their friends. If the bridegroom is a merchant, or a surgeon, or a professional man, who can only leave town for a very brief period, then, after the name may follow, " At home on the —th and —th." In the contrary case, a fresh set of cards are despatched on their return, giving the day or days on which they propose receiving their friends. As regards the style of wedding-cards, fashion is continually changing. A few years ago they were highly ornamented and fantastically tied together; now, the plainer and more unostentatious a wedding-card, the more lady-like and becoming it will be. We would particularly recommend all newly-married couples not to send their cards to any persons they do not intend to continue visiting, merely for the petty vanity of gathering a crowd, or, perhaps, for displaying their riches to astonish those for whom they have not the slightest regard or liking. It is highly discourteous to summon persons to your levee and then never return the visit. Go over your list of acquaintances, and see whom you mean to retain and whom to reject. We are not of those who blame a bride for dropping the acquaintances of her single state. Be it understood that we would regard her as ungrateful if she discarded any friend who had shown her personal kindness; but when we come to recollect that those who surround her in her girlhood's home are chiefly the friends chosen by her parents rather than herself, she ought surely to be allowed the privilege of composing her visiting list as best suits her own taste and that of her husband.

THE BRIDAL DRESS.

HIS, like all the rest of the outfit, must depend on her fortune and position in life; still, whatever be the material, it should be white. If a widow likes to wear a coloured silk, let her do so by all means, there is almost a modest propriety on her part in declining to play the bride a second time in her life; and if those of limited means prefer to choose their dress for its solidity rather than its beauty, we can but respect their economical motives, but where no such reasons exist, we cannot fancy any young maiden dressed otherwise than in white.

A Brussels lace dress over white satin, or a rich *moiré-antique* with point lace flounces would each form a beautiful costume for a bride. As to the head-dress, a veil is usually preferred, as being elegant and forming a decided costume peculiar to brides. There is something charmingly poetical in a veil and orange-flower wreath, rendered doubly attractive by its being only on one occasion through life that such a *coiffure* can be worn. The veil may be of Brussels or of point lace, or of simple *tulle* with a plain hem, each pretty in their way. The bride, with a veil, should wear an orange-

flower wreath upon her head. This flower, we may observe, which France first taught us to dedicate entirely to the service of brides, no longer holds its undivided privilege there. Jasmine, white roses, and other white flowers are now mixed up with the orthodox orange-flower wreath by some of the most eminent artificial florists of Paris.

Etiquette and Dress after Marriage.—No particular dress is required on the days the newly-married pair receive their friends. If it be winter, a rich silk or velvet dress, made high like a morning one, would be an appropriate attire for the lady. If it be summer, a light silk or barege would be suitable, but no flowers should be worn in the hair, though lace lappets and velvet bows are admissible. Wedding-cake and wine should be handed to all comers. This is generally the only form in which wedding-cake is distributed to one's friends in London. Persons in the country, not being able to assemble their friends so easily, still maintain the old custom of sending parcels of wedding-cake to all the near connections of the family; or, if they receive, pieces of cake are, nevertheless, despatched to distant friends and relatives. Some Londoners send cake to their country connections, but far the larger portion neglect this friendly old custom. Formerly, the cake was passed through the wedding ring, or the charm was not complete; but this antiquated piece of superstition is now discarded, or, at most, would only be found in existence in some old farm-house remote from town.

The visits may be returned at the end of above a week or ten days.

At the parties the young couple may attend during the first month, there is nothing inappropriate in the bride's wearing some little badge of her new state, such as a dress looped up with orange flowers or a few orange blossoms in her hair.

A new-married couple are not expected to give parties at their house for the first year; but after that time they must no longer play the part of exceptional beings, but give and take, as others.

As to the dress of a young matron, we expect it to be somewhat richer than that of an unmarried girl. The Parisians show admirable tact in the shades that distinguish the toilette of mademoiselle and madame. The girlish simplicity

hat adds a grace to the youthful attractions of the former would be out of place on the part of the latter, who, being possessed of jewels (which the French deem a superfluous ornament to the unmarried young lady), must dress in a corresponding style of luxury. Besides, she now assumes a position in society as the mistress of a house; her fate is fixed; she knows she can spend, and acts accordingly. But if the young lady, having rich parents, launches at once into the full blaze of jewels and expensive dresses, and then marries some poor captain on half-pay, she will feel humiliated at having to modify her toilette to suit her altered circumstances. This change would be less perceptible were our young ladies equally judicious with the Parisian ones, in adopting a simple style of adornment.

Should there be no settlement, and the couple be in easy circumstances, we would advise the fixing a sum for pin money, which would avoid a number of disputes, particularly among touchy people. We would advise the wife never to exceed the sum agreed upon, as some men would make that a fertile theme for expatiating on the extravagance of ladies. Many ladies prefer that their dressmaker, silk mercer, shoemaker, and others, should send in their bills to their husband, calculating that the brunt of his ill temper, if such is called forth, will fall on the tradespeople for allowing the running up of such accounts; but this is a habit that only encourages profuse expenditure where, perhaps, there is not adequate fortune to to meet it.

A cheerful home is the best security for happiness. There is not only a moral, but a physical cheerfulness that should be attended to. A well-lighted room, a neatly-served dinner, everything clean and tidy and bright, predispose the mind to pleasant impressions. Let the prudent wife strive to attain this state of things, if she values her domestic happiness.

Always receive your husband with smiles, leaving nothing undone to render home agreeable, and gratefully reciprocate his kindness and attention. Study to gratify his inclinations in regard to food and cookery, in the management of the household, in your dress, manners, and deportment. Never attempt to rule, or appear to rule, your husband. Such conduct degrades husbands, and wives always partake largely in the degradation of their husbands. In everything reasonable comply with his wishes with cheerfulness, and even, as far as possible, anticipate them. Avoid all altercations or arguments leading to ill-humour, and more especially before company. Few things are more disgusting than the altercations of the married when in the company of friends or strangers. If a lady understands that her duties are obedience, complaisance, an entire surrender of her will to that of her husband, and attention to his happiness as the first consideration, she has the spirit of the religious and civil idea of marriage.

DRESS.

MATTER of great importance in the personal economy is dress. It is necessary to health and comfort that our clothing be of proper materials; of light and soft texture, to ensure warmth without incurring fatigue; of careful adjustment to the figure; and of easy dimensions to admit of the proper play of the muscles in the various movements of the body. Dress is the criterion by which a stranger generally forms his first judgment of our taste and habits, and sometimes of our rank in society, and it, therefore, demands a proportionate degree of attention, as self-love will naturally dictate the wish to make a favourable impression. And first impressions are rarely obliterated; circumstances may occur which induce us to alter or modify our opinion; but experience in nine cases out of ten fully confirms its justice. It has been said that a tastefully dressed person carries a letter of recommendation in his or her appearance which may be read by every beholder. But nothing is graceful that outsteps the boundary of moderation; and an undue anxiety about personal decoration, to the neglect of other duties, evinces a frivolousness of character, and a mental incapacity for the cultivation of higher pursuits. The most admirable costume is not that which is most expensive, or in the extremity of the fashion; but it is that style which is best adapted to the figure, complexion, age, and circumstances of the wearer, adjusted to the person with least appearance of effort, and conveying to the mind of the observer the combined ideas of grace and comfort. A lady is ever distinguished by her minute observance of the duties of the toilette, the chasteness of her ornaments, the unaffected simplicity of her apparel, and the grace and ease of all her movements.

Now, if there are principles of true taste involved in the mysteries of a lady's toilette—and we do believe that there is a perfect style of costume adapted to every style of personal appearance—is not the study of them worthy of a refined and intellectual woman, and would not her time and thoughts be better employed in conforming her style of dress to them, than in eagerly following every change of the mode dictated by the love of novelty, apart from real beauty? We do not mean by this any wide departure from the prevailing fashion: singularity is always to be avoided. "A peculiar style of dress," says "L. E. L.," "particularly if it is becoming—and, at any rate, it will attract attention to the wearer, to the overlooking of many who are desirous to shine—will ensure for the wearer a roomful of enemies. Independence is an affront to our acquaintances." That lady is, indeed, best dressed whose costume presents an agreeable whole without anything to be remarked. Dr. Johnson once praised a lady's appearance, by saying that she was so perfectly well-dressed he could not recollect anything she had on. "It is a duty in women to dress well," continues Miss Landon ; "dress ought to be a part of female education ; her eye for colouring, her taste for draperies, from sandal to ringlet should undergo strict investigation. We should not then have our eye offended with opposite colours mixed together ; we should be spared the rigidity of form often attendant upon a new dress, and no longer behold shawls hung upon the shoulders as if upon cloak-pins in a passage."

A pure taste in dress may be gratified at a small expense ; for it does not depend upon the costliness of the materials employed, but on the just proportions observed in the forms, and an harmonious arrangement of colours. There are some rules which, being based on first principles, are of universal application, and one of those belongs to our present subject—namely, that nothing can be truly beautiful that is not appropriate. Nature and the fine arts teach that. All styles of dress, therefore, which do not sufficiently protect the person, which add unnecessarily to the heat of summer or to the cold of winter, which do not suit the age or the occupation of the wearer, or which indicate an expenditure unsuited to her means, are inappropriate and, therefore, destitute of one of the essential elements of beauty. Propriety or fitness lies at the foundation of all good taste in dressing, and to this test will every young lady possessing good sense bring a variety of obvious particulars.

It may be thought that we have placed this subject in too strong a light, but a desire to render herself agreeable by those innocent means within her reach, which may tend to cultivate and enhance her personal charms, is natural to every woman ; indeed, it is a virtuous feeling, and many valuable considerations hinge upon it ; and, so far from young ladies being taught to consider personal decoration as a matter of indifference, we believe that it may be made subservient to a higher purpose. Yet we would wish to guard against too much value being attached to it, and show how the desired end may be attained without the sacrifice of any higher good.

It is in vain that some narrow-minded religionists have endeavoured to produce in the minds of young persons an indifference to dress; or that some sects, by establishing a standard of unadorned plainness, have thought to prevent them from attaching any importance to their outward appearance. To the initiated eye even the unpretending uniform garb of the fair members of the Society of Friends presents variations of fashion; and it is possible for a young lady of that persuasion to be very much distressed by a few plaits more or less than she desired in the crown of her bonnet. Those who are restricted in form and colour can indemnify themselves by a scrupulous anxiety about texture and material. But a woman of cultivated understanding will never suffer her toilette to engross so much of her attention as to interfere with the higher duties of life, but will make it her study to acquire skill and taste to do all that is required in personal adornment with the smallest sacrifice of time, and without the appearance of consciousness or effort. Grace and elegance of attire do not require rich or splendid materials nor the " foreign aid of ornament," but a charm may be imparted to the most simple form of dress by its proper adjustment to the person, and by its harmonious blending or agreeable contrast with the other portions of the attire; and it is a truth particularly worthy of attention that a higher order of taste may be displayed and a better effect produced by a simple, unstudied, and unadorned style of dress than in the adoption of the richest decorations.

Fashion demands a discreet but not a servile observance;

much judgment may be shown in the time as well as the mode chosen for complying with her caprices. It is injudicious to adopt every new style immediately it appears, for many novelties in dress prove unsuccessful, being abandoned even before the first faint impression they produce is worn off; and a lady can hardly look more absurd than in a departed fashion, which even during its brief existence never attained a moderate share of popularity. The wearer must, therefore, at once relinquish the dress or submit to the unpleasant result we have mentioned; so that on the score of economy, as well as good taste, it is advisable not to be too eager in following the modes which whim or ingenuity create in such constant succession. On the other hand, it is unwise to linger so long as to suffer "fashion's ever-varying flower" to bud, blossom, and nearly waste its sweetness before we gather and wear it. Many persons are guilty of this error; they cautiously abstain from a too early adoption of novelty, and fall into the opposite fault of becoming its proselytes at the eleventh hour; they actually disburse as much in dress as those who keep pace with the march of mode, and are always some months behind those who are about them. Such persons labour under the further disadvantage of falling into each succeeding fashion when time and circumstances have degraded it from its "high and palmy state;" they do not copy it in its original purity, but with all the deteriorating additions which are heaped upon it subsequently to its invention. However beautiful it may be, a fashion rarely exists in its pristine state of excellence long after it has become popular, its aberrations from the perfect are exaggerated at each remove, and if its form be in some measure preserved it is displayed in unsuitable colours, or translated into inferior materials, until the original design becomes so vulgarized as to disgust.

There are many persons who, while affecting to despise

114

fashion, are always making secret compacts and compositions with her. Their constant aim is to achieve the effect of every new dress without betraying the most distant imitation of it; they pilfer the ideas of the *modiste*, which, in passing through their hands, they disfigure. By the force of habit, and by an unconscious association in the mind of a dress and its wearer, fashion, even to those who are somewhat fastidious, generally appears graceful. To please this goddess, Fashion, the fine lady of one country almost feeds herself into an apoplexy, and the would-be beauty of another starves herself into the "sister of a shade." The Chinese females cripple their feet, and the Europeans torture their waists into the narrowest possible compass. In one age she induces the fair sex to cover their faces with patches, and in the next to blush if necessity compel them to apply one; alternately to cashier, as it were, their natural tresses for false locks, to elevate their hair to immense height, or to cultivate into ringlets. General fashions should certainly be conformed to when they happen not to be repugnant to the female beauty. They may often be so modified as to suit the persons of all, and occasionally be so managed as to seem to have been created expressly for the most advantageous display of many individuals' graces of form, or delicacy of complexion. But alterations in modes must be made with considerable judgment, otherwise there is a risk of falling into absurdities. Sometimes they are altogether intractable; it is impossible so to change a fashion which has been especially invented for some tall and slender arbitress of taste that it may at once retain much of its original character, and look becoming on one whose form is either *petite* or stout. In this and similar cases the attempt should be abandoned with the consoling idea that the next mode will, in all probability, be decidedly advantageous to those who are, for the time being, debarred by Nature from appearing at once graceful and fashionable ; for the authenticity of every new edict of fashion is usually warranted by the fact of its being directly opposite in letter and spirit to its predecessor ; thus, if one year she elevate the zone to its utmost possible height, she generally depresses it in an equally unreasonable degree the next; if she prescribe evergreens for the embellishment of the hair in June, she commands summer's coronal for the same purpose in December. Should full dresses be patronized, short ladies must abstain from adopting them, because they are becoming only to the tall; and if narrow dresses obtain pre-eminence, the slender must not sacrifice that fulness in the attire for which, to them, the most exquisite display of fashion can never be a sufficient compensation. The example of those who have long necks and long shoulders should never lead those of a different style of person to wear necklaces of great breadth, to raise the dress toward the ears, or by quantity of drapery or profusion of ornament to produce an apparent union of the head-gear and the shoulders. Jewellery should never be used to cover any imperfections of form in the neck ; it is in much better taste for such a purpose to wear a neat collar reaching as high as the cheek. Those who happen to be faultless in this respect look better perhaps with the neck altogether unadorned. Whatever be the reigning mode, and however beautiful a fine head of hair may be esteemed, those who are short in stature or small in features should never indulge in a profuse display of their tresses if they would in the one case avoid the appearance of dwarfishness and unnatural size of the head, and in the other of making the face seem less than it really is, and thus causing what is only *petite* to appear insignificant.

To form the taste and improve the style of dress, a careful observation of classical figures and some of the costumes of bygone centuries will doubtless be found of considerable

115

advantage. Let not the reader imagine it is impossible to borrow hints from the attire from such sources without incurring a risk of appearing somewhat antiquated, for several of the most popular modes of the present century have been mere revivals of ancient costumes.

It is almost impossible to form a theory of the colours applicable to dress; they are subject to a thousand contingencies, and we daily discover agreeable harmonies of tint where we least expected them; and excruciating discords, produced by the juxtaposition of hues, which, from our previous experience, we were induced to believe would prove pleasing, rather than offensive. The influence of some neighbouring tint, the position of the colours combined, the relative stations, and the materials adopted for each, frequently tend to produce these effects. The colours of a single rosette often destroys the general tone and appearance of the dress, and occasionally it may be managed with such skill as to blind the tints of two or more principal parts of the costume, which, without some such mediator, would render each other obnoxious to the eye of taste. It is quite certain that the same colour which imparts a liveliness and brilliancy when used for light embellishments, and in a small quantity, becomes vulgar, showy, and disagreeable if adopted for the most extensive portion and leading tint of the attire; and, on the other hand, the delicate or neutral colours, which look well when displayed over a considerable surface, dwindle into insignificance if used in small, detached portions for minor ornaments. Generally speaking, trimmings will bear a greater richness of colour than the principal material of the dress, the breadth of which is apt entirely to subdue its decorations if they be not a little more powerful in tint. But it is a grave error to endow the minor parts of the costume with an undue superiority over the rest;

it should never be forgotten that the trimming is intended to embellish the dress, rather than that the dress should sink into a mere field for the display of the trimming; sufficient importance should always be given to the latter, so that it may enhance the beauty, add to the richness, or harmonize with the purity and neatness of the former; but if its colours be too strong, or, even when of the proper shade, if the material be too profuse, or not of a quality sufficiently delicate, it gives to the wearer either a frittered, gaudy, or coarse appearance, according to the nature of the fault. The same tint which looks well on a delicate material will not become an article which is made of "sterner stuff." The occurrence of glaring offences against good taste in the trimmings or fixed embellishments of any principal part of the attire is rare, compared with those which are perpetrated in the minor articles of gloves, shoes, ribbons, &c., which are the more important of the two, because they are not the trimmings or finishing decorations of a part, but to the whole of the costume. The former are usually left to the experience of the milliner, or copied from the production of some tasteful *modiste;* the latter depend solely on the judgment of the private individual. How often have we seen a dress, exquisite in all its parts, utterly ruined by the wearer, as a finishing touch, drawing on a vulgar glove! Much mischief of a similar nature is frequently done by feathers, flowers, ribbons, shoes, and articles of jewellery. It is not enough that a flower is pretty; it must harmonize with, or form a pleasing contrast to, the other parts of the costume, otherwise its use must be strictly forbidden. It is the same with jewellery; pearls, for instance, will suit those kinds of dresses which rubies would spoil; and the latter are appropriate in cases where the former would look faint and ineffective. Coloured shoes, we need scarcely say, are exceedingly vulgar; delicate pink and faint-blue silk, for these articles have numerous advocates; but white satin, black satin, or kid, and bronze kid, are neater and more elegant than any other colour or material. Gloves should be in the most delicate tints that can be procured; their colour has always an effect upon the general appearance. One kind of hue must not, therefore, be indiscriminately worn, or, however beautiful in itself, it may be obstinately persisted in when every other part of the attire is constantly subject to change. As it would be in bad taste for a fair young lady who is rather short in stature, however pretty she may be, if irregular as well as *petite* in her features, to take for a model in the arrangement of her hair a cast from a Greek head; so, also, would it be for one whose features are large to fritter away her hair—which ought to be kept, as much as possible, in masses of large curls, so as to subdue, or at least harmonize with, her features—into thin and meagre ringlets. Yet there is a class of features to which even these are becoming; of this we may be convinced by a glance at a collection of portraits of the period of Charles I.; unless, indeed, it be true that fine features, when ennobled by the inward light of intelligence, purity, and goodness, look well in any fashion—that they govern and give character to the style in which they are dressed, and impart a charm to, rather than receive any benefit from, either modes or ornaments. Even if this be the case, there are but few heads that possess, in a sufficient degree, the power to defy the imputation of looking absurd or inelegant if the hair be dressed in a style inconsistent with the character of the face, according to those canons of criticism which are founded upon the principles of a pure and correct taste, and established by the opinions of the most renowned painters and sculptors in every highly-civilized nation for ages past. In the arrangement of the hair, according to the shape of the face and expression of the features—in the harmonizing of the colours used in dress with the tint of the complexion—in the adaptation of form, fashion, and even material to the person—there is an ideal beauty, as well as in the figure itself; this beauty is well understood; but it is very difficult—nay, almost impossible, to describe; for it must be considered in relation to, and as modified by, the infinite varieties of form, feature, and complexion. The shades of difference are often so very minute; the inter-mixtures of different styles of persons (if this expression may be used) are so manifold; nature is so illimitable in her beautiful combination that, although we may legislate for the few, the very few who are of any decided order of form feature, or complexion, we cannot do so for the greater por-tion—the numberless individuals who, though by no means less attractive, may be said to belong to no class, but unite the peculiarities of many. It is admitted that the brunette will look best in one colour, and the blonde in another; that to the oval face a particular style of dressing the hair is most becoming; and to the elongated, a mode directly the reverse, but, in saying this, we are speaking to a comparatively small number of persons. The decidedly dark, and those of an opposite complexion, are few; it is the same with the tall and the short, those with round faces and the contrary; in each case the multitude is to be found between the two extremes. The persons composing the majority should neither adopt the specific uniform of the blonde nor the brunette—the style of dress suitable to the lofty and commanding figure, or to that of the pretty and *petite;* but modify general principles to par-ticular cases, not by producing a heterogeneous mixture of a number of different styles, but by adopting a mode which borders upon that adapted to the class to which their persons approach the nearest, without entirely losing sight of, and in some degree being governed by, their own distinguishing and specific peculiarities ; in fact, to be guided by that indispensable and ruling power in all matters connected with the toilette—taste, which, as Demosthenes said of action in relation to eloquence, is the first, second, and third grand requisite, combining the triple qualities of propriety, neatness, and elegance. By its aid the most simple materials are rendered valuable.

AT HOME.

T is said that a home without a woman in it is no home at all. It may be as neat and clean as hands can make it; it may be adorned with taste and skill; works of art, sculpture, paintings, books, even flowers, little gems of *vertu*, knick-knacks, and womanish toys—all the accessories of elegant life may be there, but at best, lacking the presence of woman, it will be only a kind of refined and luxurious museum, a dwelling-place, a shelter for the man who inhabits it when he gets weary of the society of his fellow men in the outside world; where he may, it is true, " dwell in cold *proprietus* for ever;" but where he can never know the charms, the delights of home.

But we see also in this that it is not the mere superintendence of outward surroundings, systematic arrangement, and attention to exterior comforts that is most needed in a woman, whether daughter, sister, or wife, for all these may be had with her; but if, in addition to these indispensable requisites, presiding over all, touching all with the subtle, indefinable charm of womanliness, she be there—amiable, cheerful-hearted, intelligent—this cold shadow of a home becomes a warm, living reality. Far more than this: all the luxuries of life, all its more expensive refinements, may be wanting; there may be no means to procure adornments for it; the furniture may be the plainest, the homeliest, even taste for its arrangement may be wanting; but if the woman be a true woman her home will be a bright and happy one.

The three special graces of womanhood, and the means by which she influences all around her at home and abroad, are —Love, Hope and Patience.

She must learn to be loving at home, loving with a kind, unselfish love, showing itself in little things more than in great ones. She has few opportunities there for great sacrifices, but the call for small acts of self-denial are unceasing, and a spirit of the loftiest self-sacrifice, for greater sacrifice, for greater opportunities, is often thus acquired by those who cultivate it in these "small beginnings."

It is a woman's special province to be lovingly thoughtful of the comfort of others; and it is charming to see the young girl, with this instinct of womanhood, trying to enter into the feelings of all around, to imagine their wants, and anticipate them.

Hope is but another name for cheerfulness, that, if it sees all sombre around it, looks forward brightly, and does more than look forward—tries to bring back the missing spirit of joy. It is said "If people will be good they will be happy," and we may add, "If people are happy they will be good," and it is always worth while to try the experiment. So be hopeful of and for every one. Whatever goes wrong hope and try your part to make it right; whoever errs, hope and use all your influence to lead the erring one back from the wrong path; and do all this by being yourself cheerful and trying to make all around you so. In sorrow, trouble, sickness, poverty, the presence of one hopeful-hearted woman is strength, help, and consolation to all. The very sight of a cheerful face will often drive away gloom and bitterness from a heart where they have been in full possession.

A passionate temper may cause a home tempest for awhile,

a sullen one may at times cast gloom around the fireside, but the fault-finding, repining, never-satisfied one, which goes about with a perpetual frown on the brow and pout of the lip is a ten-fold greater trial to parents, brothers, and sisters. Be cheerful then, store up sunshine in your heart, and let it beam in your face, and whatever graces of mind or body you have will be a thousandfold enhanced, while, on the other hand, if to the outside world you seem homely and lacking in every charm, to those at home you will appear all that is lovely.

As regards patience at home—if you give the matter any consideration—you will find that, first of all, it is with your own self you need to be patient. If you have any right feelings, any aspirations to be good, amiable, noble-minded, nothing will try you more than your constant shortcomings, your repeated failures to reach the standard of excellence you have set before you. In all who are striving after excellence, whether moral or mental, this standard will become higher and higher, as they add year to year, will "grow with their growth and strengthen with their strength," and so will also grow their need of patience with self.

Be patient with your family. It seems at first sight almost disrespectful to speak of patience in this connection. But, in truth, there is hardly any family relation in which it is more required.

Printed by W. WILFRED HEAD, Plough Court, FetterLane, E.C.

WARD AND LOCK'S
HUMOROUS BOOKS.

In picture wrapper, price 1s. each.

2. Artemus Ward: His Book.
3. Beeton's Riddle Book.
4. Beeton's Burlesques.
5. Beeton's Book of Charades.
6. The Biglow Papers.
7. Saxe's Poems.
8. Joe Miller's Jest Book.
9. Connubial Bliss.
16. Pusley. By C. D. WARNER.
17. Back-Log Studies. Ditto.
18. Sandy Bar. BRET HARTE.
19. Roaring Camp. Ditto.
20. The Heathen Chinee. Do.
21. Hood's Wit and Humour.
22. Whims. By THOMAS HOOD.
23. Oddities. Ditto.
24. Innocents Abroad. TWAIN.
25. The New Pilgrim's Progress. By MARK TWAIN.
26. Jerrold's Jokes and Wit.
29. Jumping Frog. M. TWAIN.
30. Letters to Punch. By ARTEMUS WARD.
31. Artemus Ward among the Mormons.
32. Naughty Jemima. Illust.
33. Eye Openers. M. TWAIN.
34. Practical Jokes. Ditto.
35. Screamers. Ditto.
36. Awful Crammers.
37. Babies and Ladders, by EMANUEL KINK, and Artemus Ward among the Fenians.
38. Holmes' Wit and Humour.
39. Josh Billings: His Sayings.
40. The Danbury Newsman.
41. The Mystery of Mr. E. Drood. By ORPHEUS C. KERR.
42. Shaving Them.
43. Mr. Brown on the Goings-on of Mrs. Brown.
44. Sensation Novels. By BRET HARTE.
46. Mr. Sprouts: His Opinions.
48. The Ramsbottom Papers.

49. Major Jack Downing.
50. The Pagan Child, and other Sketches. By BRET HARTE.
51. Helen's Babies. By JOHN HABBERTON. Illustrated.
52. The Barton Experiment. By Author of "Helen's Babies."
53. The Mississippi Pilot. By MARK TWAIN.
54. The Jericho Road. By the Author of "Helen's Babies."
55. Some Other Babies, very like Helen's, only more so.
56. The Story of a Honeymoon. By C. H. Ross. Illust.
57. That Dreadful Boy Trotty.
58. Hans Breitmann's Ballads.
59. Other People's Children. Sequel to, and by the Author of "Helen's Babies." Illustrated.
60. Cent. per Cent. B. JERROLD.
61. That Husband of Mine.
62. Two Men of Sandy Bar. By BRET HARTE.
63. Grown-up Babies. Author of "Helen's Babies." Illustrated.
64. Other People. Ditto.
65. Folks in Danbury.
66. My Wife's Relations.
67. My Mother-in-Law.
68. Babbleton's Baby.
69. The Scripture Club of Valley Rest. JOHN HABBERTON.
70. That Girl of Mine.
71. Bessie's Six Lovers.
72. Mark Twain's Nightmare. With Tales, Sketches and Poetry by MARK TWAIN, F. C. BURNAND, H. S. LEIGH, &c., and Illustrations by LINLEY SAMBOURNE, A. B. FROST, &c.
73. Bret Harte's Hoodlum Band, and other Stories.
74. Bret Harte's Deadwood Mystery. With Tales and Sketches by F. C. BURNAND and others. Illustrated by JOHN PROCTOR, &c.

London: WARD, LOCK & CO., Salisbury Square, E.C.